# RANGDA

## THE LEGENDARY GODDESS OF BALI

## BRANDON SPARS

*Illustrated by*
CLARA SPARS

WAYZGOOSE PRESS

Edited by Maggie Sokolik

Front cover design and illustrations by Clara Spars

Back cover design by DJ Rogers, Book Branders

ISBN: 978-1938757822

# CONTENTS

*This work is dedicated by the author and the illustrator to Putu Irmawati, loving wife and mother, and all women of Bali.*

# NOTES ON THE SPELLING OF BALINESE AND JAVANESE NAMES

While researching the texts for this book, especially transliterations of the lontar literature behind the epic *Calon Arang*, there was a wide variety of different spellings for the names of different historical figures and characters. The eleventh century king of Daha, for example, was spelled Erlangga in Pramoedya's prose version of the sixteenth century Javanese manuscript, as well as the scholar I Made Suastika's treatment of the Balinese texts. Meanwhile the king's name is spelled "Airlangga" by other scholars and writers, and a modern university in Surabaya is named after this patron of arts and learning with this spelling. While I frequently hear and read the epithet "Walu Nateng Dirah" for the principal character Calon Arang, which means the "widow from the village of Dirah," Swastika's transliteration of the lontar texts uses the spelling "Girah" (as does Pramoedya's prose version) for this village located on the outskirts of Erlangga's kingdom. Therefore, in this work wherever possible, I will use that spelling. As for the priest, the protagonist of the sixteenth century lontar prose version of the story, there have been multiple transliterations not only for his name, but also for his priestly title. The title "Mpu," which Suastika notes is an indication of brahmin, priestly status, has been spelled "Empu" elsewhere (even in Pramoedya's prose version). His name, which Suastika transliterates as "Baradah," has been also spelled "Bharadah" and "Bahrada" elsewhere. For the sake of consistency, I will therefore stick to Suastika's spellings, which are derived from his scholarly treatment of two Balinese lontar manuscripts: *Calon Arang* Prosa LOr 5387/5279 and *Geguritan Calon Arang* Kirtya 1047. Therefore the list of characters, wherever possible, will be spelled as follows:

*King Erlangga*: the eleventh century king of Kadiri (which is also referred to by its capital Daha); Erlangga was succeeded by his two sons who divided the kingdom into Kadiri and Janggala.

*Mpu Baradah*: priest at the ashram in Lemah Tulis

*Wedawati*: daughter of Mpu Baradah

*Mpu Bahula*: student of Mpu Baradah who marries Ratna Manggali

*Calon Arang*: the widow in the village of Girah, referred to often in Bali today as "Walu Nateng Dirah," who practices witchcraft and sends a plague upon the kingdom of Daha. This figure forms the historical basis for Rangda's identity, while her religious and mythical origins are linked to the Hindu deities, Uma and Durga.

*Ratna Manggali*: the daughter of Calon Arang

*Siwa*: the Indonesian, Balinese, and Javanese spelling of the Hindu deity Shiva

*Wisnu*: the Indonesian selling for the Hindu deity Vishnu

*Durga*: the mythological origins of Rangda, also linked to Uma in two Balinese texts *Kalatattwa* and *Siwagama* (in both Siwa curses Uma to become Durga)

# AUTHOR'S INTRODUCTION

The Balinese masked character, Rangda, has captured my imagination for most of my life. At different times, she has inspired different feelings ranging from fear and awe to love and fondness. She defies description and analysis. That is perhaps the only true statement that I can make about her.

The first time I saw Rangda was late at night at a Barong dance ceremony in a village temple. I can't even remember where it was, but I do remember the gas lanterns hanging on either end of the *kalangan* or stage in the outer courtyard of the temple. Incense rose in enormous clouds, and in the smoke stood Rangda facing off with the Barong. She held him by the beard with one hand, the other was raised high in the air, the six-inch fingernails the player wears casting eerie shadows on the courtyard wall. In the flickering light shone hundreds of frightened eyes as the congregation looked on, pressed in just a few feet from where Rangda and the Barong stood.

I started my young adulthood with the intention of becoming a scholar who would have the luxury of spending my days studying

Rangda and the vast repertoire of folklore and religion surrounding her, but my love of teaching led me down the path of secondary education rather than to the ivory tower. As a high school teacher, my deepest passion manifested itself: storytelling. So now, I do have the luxury of spending my days recreating myths and legends for my ninth grade students, mingling them with personal anecdotes when I can, and encouraging students to tell their own stories.

Teaching high school did not end my love for or my fascination with Rangda. I teach a unit on the history and the culture of Indonesia, and, of course, the legends, myths, and beliefs about this goddess form part and parcel of my lessons about purification rituals. While Indonesia is actually the largest Muslim country in the world, Islam making up the faith that ninety percent of the population ascribes to, Bali has remained Hindu. Prior to the arrival of Islam and the establishment of the Mataram Empire, Indonesia was host to various Hindu and Buddhist empires such as the kingdoms of Sailendra, which produced the Buddhist monument known as Borobudur, Sanjaya, a rival kingdom which produced Prambanan, and Majapahit, which may have held most of Southeast Asia under its influence in the thirteenth and four-teenth centuries. Meanwhile, along the East Coast of Sumatra and the North Coast of Java, Muslim kingdoms began to develop and gain power, often only trading with each other. Hindu/Buddhist hegemony over the island of Java was eventually ended in 1478 when Demak sacked Majapahit and established the Islamic kingdom of Mataram. Bali, however, remained free of the Islamic influence, even though centuries later when Indonesian independence was declared the Hinduism of Bali was not officially acknowledged as an official religion because of its animistic and polytheistic appearances. While Bali constitutes a small minority in Indonesia, it has often been the focus of scholars simply because it is considered to be a window to pre-Islamic Indonesia, having preserved traditions and narratives such as those surrounding Rangda.

I married a woman from Canggu, Bali, and we have been going back as often as we can to spend time with her family, and to bring our two children to visit the people and live on the island that make up half of their identities. There was no greater joy for me than to see that Rangda completely captivated them as well. And now I have the pleasure of collaborating with my daughter on this book, the aim of which is to share our appreciation of this complex and imaginative goddess.

This book has three parts. In the first part I examine the different narratives associated with Rangda, with close attention to her roots in eleventh century history as well as within Hindu mythology. The written narratives differ quite a bit from the more casual interpretations of ritual performances in which the plots of the stories of Rangda are sometimes only present in traces, or, at best, merely suggested. The face to face exchanges between Rangda and the Barong are, however, always highlighted and emphasized, occupying the crux of the ritual performances. Seldom is there a clear resolution to their altercation, which has led some scholars, such as Margaret Mead, to state that the fight between good and evil continues eternally. Most Balinese, however, do not see Rangda as representative of evil, or the Barong, good. As we will see in the discussions that follow, their identities are far more complex than that. The lack of a resolution to their altercation has been explained to me rather that they exist eternally in the ocean, something I heard from the students I was teaching in the 1990s and again by people I met while doing research on Rangda. As I mention later, this association with the ocean is in keeping with Rangda's role as the guardian of the village, which she accomplishes by cleansing the village of impurity, pollution, corruption, disease, and death. In this way she embodies the downstream quality of water in its ability to carry away the remains of burnt

offerings as well as trash and garbage. Paired with Rangda's affilia-
tion with downstream water is the upstream purity and fertility,
which are associated with both the Rice Goddess, Dewi Sri, and
the Goddess of the Lake, Dewi Danau.

The final part of this book examines the dynamic of the rituals,
which is how Rangda is most often experienced by Balinese. The
research for this portion of the book was conducted in the 1990s
nearing the end of the New Order rule of President Suharto.
During these years, there was a deep transformation taking place
in the construction of the Balinese stage, which was once simply a
designated area known as a *kalangan*, and has slowly given way to
a western sense of a stage, much more separated from the audience, known as a *panggung*. As is pointed out in the third part, this
transformation is aligned with the introduction of "print oriented"
traditions to what was largely an "orally oriented" society. It
should be noted that even the lontar manuscripts discussed in part
one were seldom perused privately but were more commonly read
aloud to audiences, or in small groups, and were therefore
consumed orally. The transformation due to film and print literature, as I discuss, not only changes the performances, but also
impacts the narratives themselves and how they are interpreted.

Some of this book may tend toward academia and not a general
readership, but that is a consequence of my attempt to help my
audience appreciate the complexity of Rangda. Therefore my
reader may have to slog through the more dense sections, but I am
confident that the fascination and the appeal that Rangda will have
on them will be enough to carry them through. The illustrations of
my daughter, while limited to the storytelling portion of this book,
should set the tone for the entire work. Therefore I encourage the
reader to refer to them frequently while reading this!

## ILLUSTRATOR'S INTRODUCTION

I grew up navigating two sides of my identity and how they both complemented and collided with one another: my mother's side of the family is rooted in Bali, Indonesia, where they all live to this day, while my father's side, in California.

There is and always has been a vibrant, occasionally intimidating, energy that permeates throughout the island of Bali—from its tropical plants, from its towering temples, from the rituals that take place from one village to the next, from the strong sense of community. It was this very energy that attracted the curiosity and eventual affection of my father when he first left his Californian life behind to venture out to Indonesia, and it is this same energy that creates a puzzling sense of emptiness in my comfortable life in America: I feel the pull of my Balinese heritage grow stronger with every passing day.

I've been drawing in my free time since middle school, but it wasn't until recently that I began to use art as a means of exploring the interaction between the two cultures that I call my own. I founded a small business called KITA Products, which features these drawings and designs printed onto clothing, stickers, and other accessories. "Kita" is the Indonesian word for "us." This word seemed to be an adequate representation of the sense of unity I wanted to inspire with my designs.

It wasn't long after I created KITA that my father suggested that I illustrate his next book devoted to the goddess, Rangda. This was a perfect way for me to link my heritage with my love for visual art and design.

Though I usually complete all of my drawing on paper with pen and ink, for these illustrations I have used digital means to create finer details and deeper contrasts. Each picture implements bold contour lines, pointillistic shading, Balinese-style imagery, and the same black and white graphic aesthetic.

This book serves as the culmination of many things: my own stylistic exploration of contemporary American art with traditional Balinese imagery, the academic and personal depiction of my American father's experience of my mother's world, and ultimately, the two sides of my identity and family history merging through both art and storytelling.

I hope that the result of this cross-cultural interaction resonates with and touches others who are facing their own internal examinations of identity and family. It has certainly helped me make some sense of my own.

# PART I
---
# TEXTUAL TRADITIONS OF RANGDA

# THE MASK OF RANGDA

Various scholars over the years have tried to pin Rangda down and analyze her, but each interpretation has given way to a new one beginning with Margaret Mead and Gregory Bateson in the 1930s to Clifford Geertz in the 1950s and 1960s to leading modern scholars like J. Stephen Lansing and Adrian Vickers. Of course this is not to mention the leading Balinese scholar, I Made Bandem, who has written on dance, drama, and the arts extensively, or I Made Suastika, who produced an in-depth analysis of the lontar tradition surrounding the premier epic that features Rangda, *The Calon Arang*. My own research touched on Rangda when I was a graduate student at UC Berkeley where I produced a Master's thesis, which is the basis for the third part of this book. I married a Balinese woman, whose relatives were the priests for the village temple in Babakan, Canggu where Rangda made regular appearances.

Describing Rangda has always focused on her horrific appearance, with bulging eyes, exposed tusks, sagging dugs, and the coils of intestines that sway like salamis hanging in a butcher shop as she twirls, hops, and jigs with sudden jerks. The mask is elaborate, carved from a special tree said to be inhabited by Siwa's and Uma's monstrous, aborted child (Stephen "Barong" 161). Rimming the bulbous eyes is leather carved into leafy flames, repeated at the crown of her head, and at the corners of her mouth. Real boars' tusks protrude from her forehead as if she is bristling with dangerous energy, and a tongue is unfurled even lower than the sagging flaps of skin that were once breasts. The contradiction between her sprite movements and the sagging flesh and overgrown hair is a disarming display of post-reproductive femininity, commanding of men and women alike. She bears the wisdom of having given life, suckled many children, and undoubtedly buried many as well, while she herself seems to have transcended the span of a regular life. All together her features make her simultaneously mortal and eternal, and such are the details of her origins: she is both historical and mythical.

# HISTORICAL TRADITION

In history she is known as *Walu Nateng Dirah*, or "the Widow from the Village of Girah," which is located in East Java during the eleventh century. Without a husband, she raised a daughter, Ratna Manggali, who, though beautiful, could not find a willing suitor. All were afraid of her mother, who was rumored to be quite knowledgeable in black magic. The great modern Indonesian novelist, Pramoedya Ananta Toer, produced a prose version of the legend, which recounts the struggle of King Erlangga to quell the plague produced by this witch and restore peace and prosperity to his realm. Originally published in 1951 in Indonesian, the prose novella was translated into English by William Samuels in 2002 under the title *The King, The Witch, and The Priest* after there became a renewed interest in the story (to be discussed later). As Heather Curnow notes in her Ph.D. thesis, the source for the story seems to be a sixteenth century tantric Javanese manuscript. Pramoedya, according to Curnow, perpetuates the version of the narrative that dramatizes the triumph of patriarchal state power over uncontrolled female, creative energy, which it presents as destructive and immoral.

I Made Suastika's work, *Calon Arang dalam Tradisi Bali*, focuses on the Balinese lontar tradition (palm leaf manuscripts) which underpins the legend, its transmission, and its transformation from the Javanese original. Suastika transliterates *Calon Arang* Prosa LOr 5387/5279, an early prose version produced in Bali during the Gelgel Dynasty in 1540, and then translates this into modern Indonesian. Suastika then does the same with a more recent lontar, *Geguritan Calon Arang* Kirtya 1047, a poetic version of the legend produced during the nineteenth century Klungkung Dynasty by Anak Agung Gde Pameregan who lived from 1810 to 1892. In his comparison of the two lontar texts, Suasitika examines a process that Theodore G. Th. Pigeaud labeled "Balinization" in his seminal text *Literature of Java*.

During the Gelgel Dynasty, in the early sixteenth century, especially under the powerful king Waturenggong, according to Suastika, two literary forms were deployed. Both in service of validating the authority and legitimacy of priestly authority within the court, the *kidung* is the Balinese poetic rendition of the Javanese *kakawin* while *sastra prosa* or "literary prose" was the fofrm devoted to chronicling historical events. *Calon Arang* Prosa LOr 5387/5279 is a prose text written in Middle Javanese, or *Jawa Pertengahan*, which is also called *Kawi-Bali* (Suastika 307). Javanese influence on Bali became unavoidable when the Majapahit Empire of East Java occupied Bali in 1343. Suastika writes (my translation from the Indonesian):

> After Ratna Asura Bumi Banten, a royal descendant of Warmadewa [founder of a ninth and tenth century dynasty in Bali] died in 1332, a Majapahit expedition arrived in 1343 with the goal of placing Bali under its control. The efforts of the Majapahit leader Gajah Mada to force Bali into submission did not dispel the atmosphere of chaos in Bali at the time in spite of Gajah Mada's having placed *ksatrian* rulers in charge. The

campaign revealed that the true nature of Majapahit rule was by force rather than friendship or family. The original Balinese inhabitants (*orang Bali Aga*) wanted to hold onto their existence by formally accepting the continued rule of the King of Kadiri [Java].

One individual from the Bali Aga named Patih Ulung from Bedahulu (Tampak Siring) was willing to go to Majapahit to try to end the chaos in Bali (*Babad Arya Kutawaringin,* 1.14). He asked to meet with the Vice Regent of Majapahit, Gajah Mada, about the chaos in Bali. In their discussion, Majapahit accepted the suggestion made by the Balinese people who were loyal to Kadiri (Daha). Sri Mpu Kresna Kepakisan, who had a connection to Daha's lineage, was recruited to carry out the Majapahit mission in Bali...

With the installment of the new king, the palace was moved from Samprangan near the city of Gianyar to Gelgel in Klungkung (Gde Agung, 1989: 22). The move of the palace and the arrival of the nobles from the Island of Java actually didn't result in the loss of all the Old Balinese traditions from Semprangan or Bedahulu that had developed over the previous four centuries. Remnants of the literary and cultural traditions lived on...

After the move of the kingdom to Gelgel, courtly works of literature began to appear, which are the acclaimed, aesthetic works of Bali. Those writers continued the Old Javanese traditions, which included producing works of prose. Reworkings of the Javanese texts called *kidung* and *babad* were created, which are works of poetry and prose containing historical elements. The possibility cannot be ruled out that the Javanese influence in the Gelgel was not the result of the arrival of religious figures from the Island of Java... (303-306)

Among those religious figures purported to have arrived in Bali is none other than Mpu Baradah, a historical figure who is featured as a principal character in *The Calon Arang*.

In this prose lontar, Mpu Baradah forms the sacred focus of the text. The text features the building of the bond between the priestly figure of Mpu Baradah and that of the ruler, King Erlangga, who ruled in Daha, Java during the eleventh century. The text features many discourses and the establishment of protocol between the king and his "older brother," the priest, which Suastika observes may have had significance in the establishment of this very relationship during the Gelgel Dynasty between the king and the *Siwa-Buda* priests. The older brother/younger brother relationship outlined in this text served as a model not only for demarcating authority over religious matters but also over policy. In a key scene of the Balinese lontar, not included in Pramoedya's retelling of the Javanese manuscript, Mpu Baradah is consulted by the king on how his two sons are to succeed him. King Erlangga's inclination is to allow one son to rule Java, and one to rule Bali. Mpu Baradah, however, causes the king to pause before he passes such a decree, whereupon the priest travels to Bali and meets with another priest, Mpu Kuturan. In a contest of supernatural power between the two, Mpu Kuturan convinces Mpu Baradah not to allow King Erlangga to install his son as Bali's ruler, whereupon Mpu Baradah returns to Daha. There he advises the king to divide the rule of Java between the two: one in Kadiri and the other in Janggala. The episode may be a result of the author's attempt to model and nuance the delicate relationship between the priestly caste (*brahmana*) and the ruling caste (*ksatria*), which was resettling as a result of the shift in power due to Javanese intervention.

The central argument of Suastika's book is that the reworking of the Javanese story from the prose version of the Gelgel Dynasty to the nineteenth century poetic version of the Klungkung Dynasty was a result of the relationship between literature and the court. By the nineteenth century literature was moved outside the purview of the courts and had been reoriented in its purpose, which was rearranged for the entertainment and moral betterment of the commoner. Suastika writes (my translation from Indonesian):

*Calon Arang* LOr 5387/5279 is a work of literature born of the Karangasem tradition. This text was created in retreats or ashrams by ascetic religious figures. The name of the location where this text was produced is Smadri Camara in Karangasem. *Calon Arang* was written to pass on the magical value of the clan to its future generations. The contents were revised during the historical context of the sixteenth century in Bali when the political climate was unstable. During that time there was a "Javanization" of the Balinese court on the one hand, while on the other there arose in the Bali Aga (indigenous Balinese inhabitants) a demand for justice, freedom, and the ability to continue to practice their religious beliefs in Siwa and Tantric Buddhism, which formed the essence of Balinese culture at that time.

From the thematic perspective of *Calon Arang* LOr 5387/5279, we find a close tie to Siwa-Tantric Buddhism, which is a religious current developed from early Balinese times. The function of *Calon Arang* is to provide direction for cleansing rituals. The cruelty of Calon Arang aided by her disciples with black magic deriving its power from the books and written documents (*pustaka, lipyakarya*) in her possession caused people in Daha to die. Mpu Baradah, a Buddhist priest, saved the kingdom from ruin. He exorcised Calon Arang so she was free from sin and revealed the path and the teachings to other characters to achieve liberation (*kalepasan*). Eventually, all the characters received sacred teachings from the priest Baradah along with the happiness of release (*moksa namu-namu mur*)...

Based on the theme and function, *Calon Arang* LOr 5387/5279 can be located within the tradition of Bali. This text was born in the atmosphere of an ashram. With this in mind, we should remember that ashrams (*geria*) were the centers for cleansing in Bali. These cleansings were performed by high priests of both Siwa and Buddha, ascetics, master puppeteers, and regular priests. *Calon Arang* and other texts bearing the theme of purification and cleansing gave direction for guiding the cleansing process... These works were transplanted from the ashram to the secular world of Bali including the palace...

Moving along, the function of *Geguritan Calon Arang* Kirtya 1047 is aesthetic (for pleasure), in which we find general discourse about religious values, such as *utpeti, stiti, pralina,* and questions of *Ong kara* to *Dasaksara.* Yet, all this merely forms the content, which is wrapped within aesthetic elements, especially the usage of the Kawi-Bali language in *sinom* and *pangkur* rhythms. The writer comments on the function of the text in the following...

III.108 Forgive me for imitating a song, especially the literary experts, because it would be stupid and vain for me to imitate the expert writers when my intention is to lift heavy hearts.

We may conclude, in accordance with our analysis above, the theme of *Geguritan Calon Arang* is that of a religious aesthetic work written for its beauty and its dialogs on religion and culture in Bali. With respect to its ambitious aims to both preserve ancient knowledge while maintaining the literary ability to free individuals from heaviness of heart, this work contains a valuable blend of teachings and aesthetics. Thus there is a change in function from guiding purification and cleansing rituals to entertaining the reader. (358-360)

The impact of the transformation from a religious text to a popular aesthetic one is felt in the plot and the characters. Much of the historical context surrounding the kingdom of Daha is absent in the poem. For example, the division of the realm into two halves, Janggala and Kadiri, is missing, which is an indication of the different role played by the poem. Relieved of its purpose in rhetorically demonstrating the hegemony the priestly caste held over the rulers (*brahmana* over *ksatria*), Suastika notes how the witch plays the central role, rather than the priest. In the prose version, the priest is spotlighted in his role conducting ceremonies, advising the king on how to proceed, and teaching his students the dharma. The relationship of an older sibling to a younger one between the priest and the king is not emphasized or discussed, and rather than the redeemer of the witch, the priest plays more of a role akin to an assassin (349). The witch, on the other hand, is much more of a thrilling villain, her dark assemblies in the cemetery with her disciples eclipsing the pedantic discourses between the priest and the king, the priest and his students, and even the priest with the witch. Perhaps most importantly, in the *Geguritan Calon Arang*, Mpu Baradah executes the Calon Arang without having cleansed her of her sin or redeemed her. In the prose version of the story, Calon Arang formed an alter ego to Mpu Baradah, in that he too was the widowed parent of a daughter, he too had numerous students, and, finally, he too spent time in the graveyard where his daughter had taken up residence in her selfless service tending to her mother's grave and all the dead. Whereas she practices the knowledge in the sacred book she possesses from left to right, Mpu Baradah undoes her spells by reading them from right to left. Her execution without redemption, according to Suastika, reveals the deep change in her symbolism, from representing the opposite of dharma (*adharma*) in the prose version to simply embodying the "six deadly sins" of the common people at that time: "Rangda deceives, rages, poisons, slanders, destroys, and protests (*neluh*)" (350).

Pramoedya's retelling of the story in modern Indonesian prose begins with a vision of a prosperous kingdom: "The kingdom was a populous one and its people very prosperous. Harvests were always bountiful for the kingdom was free of vermin and pestilence" (9). However, the tension arises immediately with the introduction of the widow: "Throughout the kingdom this village had a much-feared reputation because in it lived a witch by the name of Calon Arang... Calon Arang was a woman of some years in age with a daughter by the name of Ratna Manggali. Now this young woman was astoundingly fair of face but at the ripe age of twenty-five was still unmarried. It is said that such was their fear of her mother, no eligible suitors dared to ask for her hand" (15). This tension develops simply and steadily: "And so it was because everyone disliked her, Calon Arang's anger and her enmity toward her fellow man continued to grow" (17).

Pramoedya parallels the rise of the villain with that of the hero of the story, Mpu Baradah, who teaches numerous students at his ashram in Lemah Tulis. Mpu Baradah has a beautiful daughter as well, Wedawati, who is transformed by her mother's death from the beautiful spark of joy in the village to a despondent, selfless devotee to her father's faith, destined, like Ratna Manggali at first, for a life of solitude in service of her lone parent. The parallels pit the guided temperance of Mpu Baradah with the self-indulgent thirst for power and revenge of the witch, and this is underscored by her ability to spread plague, pestilence, and death, which is countered by the priest's ability to heal, cleanse, and resurrect the dead.

The Calon Arang frequently gathers with her disciples in the graveyard of Girah, where they perform sacrifices and wild dances for the goddess Durga, who appears and grants them tremendous powers to spread pestilence and plague. The effects on the realm are felt immediately and are compounded when Calon Arang summons Durga a second time to gain permission to spread the plague to members of the court itself.

In Pramoedya's version, the king first attempts to capture Calon Arang, but the very same army that had brought other kingdoms to their knees proved ineffective against Daha's own witch. In an eerie scene a commander triumphantly charges across the kingdom to Girah with his battalion, but then one by one as soldiers enter the home to confront Calon Arang as she sleeps on her bed, they are burned to ashes.

Meanwhile, Wedawati has become the object of Mpu Baradah's new wife's jealousy. After a bitter quarrel with her stepmother, Wedawati retires to the graveyard to tend to her mother's grave and provide rites for all of the corpses that begin to arrive as a result of the Calon Arang's black magic. The great degree of stoic mourning of the bereft Wedawati in the Lemah Tulis graveyard measures the degree to which the blood-soaked trances of Calon Arang and her students in the graveyard at Girah are at variance in the opposite moral direction.

Mpu Baradah's advice to King Erlangga is simple: give the widow what she wants. The sage sends his greatest student, Bahula, along with an enormous dowry from the king to marry Ratna Manggali, but although Calon Arang is pleased and flattered by her handsome, wealthy son in law, the plague continues relentlessly, which requires Mpu Baradah to enact his ulterior motive for the marriage: to obtain the book containing the witch's powerful mantras. Once Bahula obtains the book for his teacher, Mpu Baradah journeys to Girah, healing the sick and raising the dead as he goes:

> Calon Arang immediately turned towards a distant banyan tree and blew towards it. Fire jumped from her mouth to the tree and

the tree burst into a ball of flames. A moment later the tree was nothing but a pile of smoking ambers.

"Now do you believe me?" the woman screamed at him. "Now do you see what I can do?"

Mpu Baradah spoke to Calon Arang as if to a small child. "Please, now I'd like to see what you can really do."

"Are you making fun of me?" Calon Arang hissed. "You little shrimp of a priest!"

"Oh, no, I'm serious," Mpu Baradah told her. "I really would like to see a display of real power."

The Priest's challenge fanned Calon Arang's anger. Her breath rose and fell. Beads of sweat appeared on her temples and trickled downwards to her chest. She then opened her mouth and blew towards him. A large flame leapt from her mouth and wrapped itself around the Priest but he remained untouched and unscathed by the heat and flames.

Calon Arang continued to blow flames towards the Priest but he remained standing quietly before her as if nothing were happening. She roared like a lion as the fire burned. She increased the size of the flame but not even a hair on Mpu Baradah's head was singed.

Seeing that the Priest remained unscathed, Calon Arang could hardly control herself. Her anger caused her teeth to change into fangs; her body curled into a hump. The hairs on her head stood erect like the feathers of a fighting cock. (113-114)

The patriarchal notes hit here in the retelling actually begin with Mpu Baradah's arrival in Girah when Calon Arang immediately begs to be cleansed of her sins. Shaking his head as if to a child who doesn't understand either the gravity or the consequences of her actions, Mpu Baradah explains to her that she must pay for her sins with her life, which produces her childlike tantrum described above. When she is finished shooting fire and screaming, Mpu Baradah takes her life effortlessly only, upon reconsidering, to bring her back so that she might be absolved of her sins first and then die:

> Calon Arang's heart leapt with joy. Her sins were so great but even she could find forgiveness. She realized that only the holiest of people could ever erase the scourge from her soul.
>
> Mpu Baradah then spoke to Calon Arang, the widow from Girah, about the virtues of goodness. His lesson enlightened the woman and her aware of her crimes and the evil of her deeds. The knowledge brought her great happiness and she bowed to Mpu Baradah as a sign of obeisance.
>
> Weksirsa and Mahisa Wadana [her disciples] also learned from the Priest and the foul traits that had been in them also vanished. There and then they pledged themselves to Mpu Baradah and his cause and, as time would eventually show, they became two of the most loyal and faithful students he had ever had.
>
> After imparting the wisdom to Calon Arang, Mpu Baradah then returned her to her lifeless state. She was at peace now; her soul had vanished and, with it, the danger that her life had previously meant for the people of Daha. (115-116)

Mpu Baradah instructs not only those depraved individuals who had fallen under Calon Arang's influence, but also the king himself, and the epic ends with a vision of harmony even greater than that at the outset prior to Calon Arang's attack:

> Armed with the knowledge that King Erlangga obtained from
> Mpu Baradah, he then began to improve the welfare of the people,

for which he came to be most loved. Even those countries he conquered were pleased to have him for their sovereign. People from China and India freely came to Java's shores to trade. Commerce thrived and was profitable for all parties concerned. New ships were built and the rivers and the coasts were full of trading vessels. The end result was a happier and more prosperous people.

Children played in the city square once more. They grazed their animals in pastures without fear. Now that Calon Arang and the mysterious illness were gone no one felt fear anymore. Few people died untimely deaths. As it should be, most people died of old age. Farmers tilled their fields and harvests were bountiful; no one feared hunger any more. Such was the state of the kingdom of Daha after the death of Calon Arang. (121-122)

Bahula and Ratna Manggali remained happily married, and then, in an epilogue, we are told that Mpu Baradah, in his old age, leaves his ashram to his son by his second wife. On a mystical note, he disappears into the hills accompanied only by his daughter, Wedawati. The two are never seen or heard from again.

As Curnow states in her dissertation, the moral of the story told in the Javanese manuscript and in Pramoedya's retelling is that state power and religious authority triumph over "the dark and subversive powers of the feminine" (32). We might imagine the role that traditional texts such as the Javanese manuscript played in reinforcing the authority and legitimacy of the ruler, who is presented as a beneficent patriarch in opposition to the angry, vengeful, and dangerous forces that are wielded by the widow, whose transgressions represent the risks that women pose when outside the structure of a marriage or the watchful eye of a father. Ratna Manggali's ambivalence toward her mother, how she both loves her but also knows she is deserving of punishment by King Erlangga's state, is linked to the lack of a father, and, once married and possessive of moral clarity, she actively participates in bringing about her own mother's downfall. This is contrasted with Wedawati, who, though motherless, has the tutelage of her kind father. The patriarchal knowledge she receives from her father has made the guiding presence of a husband unnecessary in her case.

The Kingdom of Erlangga (Daha) is treated quite favorably by Indonesian history. When we study this kingdom in my ninth grade classes, it is often treated as a kind of golden age (second only to the greatness of Majapahit, which would arise also in East Java two centuries later). King Erlangga is associated with the arts, and it is under his rule that writing was brought to Indonesia presumably from India. Hindu and Buddhist scholars from both China and India lived in the courts, and the arts for which Indonesia has become famous—gamelan and shadowplay—were fostered by the king. Therefore it seems quite natural that one of the most famous of the epic tales indigenous to Indonesia would be set during the rule of this most beneficent and enlightened king.

# MYTHOLOGICAL AND RELIGIOUS TRADITION

It might not actually be possible to pin down the narrative in which Rangda appears to face off with the Barong, or, perhaps it might be best to simply say that the masked encounter that is dramatized daily for tourists and at the very least bi-annually in the Pura Dalem of every Balinese village contains many layers of narrative that are simultaneously being told. The encounter between the Barong and Randa is the climax of two different rituals: the Calon Arang and the Barong. Both of these rituals are performed as village cleansing ceremonies, and both feature Rangda in her face off with the Barong. The Barong dance normally does not include the characters Mpu Baradah or Ratna Manggali, although Spies and de Zoete note that it occasionally does (Spies 102). Conversely, just as the Barong dance, which would normally reference the more mythical and religious origins of the Barong/Rangda encounter, can also reference the historical context, we find that according to Michele Stephen, the legend of Calon Arang can be interpreted from a religio-mythical perspective, with the character of Mpu Baradah being identified with Siwa, and Calon Arang as Durga (Stephen "Returning" 89).

Michele Stephen in his two articles "Barong and Rangda in the Context of Balinese Religion" and "Returning to Original Form" brings the mythical narrative to the forefront of his interpretation of the dance drama involving the masked characters. Stephen's interpretation links the narrative told in the dance to the function of the ritual itself, which is to cleanse and purify the village. The impurity and pollution brought about by Rangda and her disciples (known as *sisya*) is rectified by the Barong, who represents Siwa, who has followed Uma to earth after cursing her to become Durga. On earth, Siwa takes the demonic form of the Barong.

One of the creation stories forming the context for the encounter between Siwa and Uma (as Barong and Rangda) is told in the Hindu text titled, "The Litany of the Resi Bhujangga," which was collected and translated by the famous Dutch scholar Christiaan Hooykaas (Stephen 165). Stephen summarizes the text as follows:

> The account of the creation of the world begins with the emergence of the goddess Uma from the ankles of Siwa to become his spouse. Together the divine pair created the gods Kosika, Garga, Maitri, Kurusya and Prantanjala. When the "Upper World" was complete, the gods were sent down to create the world. They were cursed by Siwa, then Kosika sprang off to the east and took the form of a demon, Maitri sprang off to the west and took the form of a snake, Kurusya sprang to the north and took the form of a crocodile, while Prantanjala sprang to the center and became King of the Turtles. Prantanjala descended to help create the world with the goddess Uma. The goddess fixes her mind in concentration and from the sweat of her body issued the goddess Ganga, and then from the dried salt of Uma's sweat falling into the Ganga appeared the goddess Ocean. The Earth goddess appeared, but is as yet only 'one turf's width." Uma meditated again and began to create the whole world, The Sun, The Moon and Stars and Planets came forth, the Five Coarse Elements (Panca

Mahabhuta) came forth and then the four elements, the Water, Light, Wind and Sky. The Three Worlds were complete and "all was ordered," "all was arranged." (165-166)

At this point, Stephen stops to analyze a change that comes over Uma as she surveys her own accomplishments. Having created everything, she now transforms into her more terrible aspect, Durga. Stephen quotes Hooykaas' text:

> *Her teeth were long and sharp, like tusks,*
> *Her mouth an abyss in between,*
> *Her eyes shown, they were like twin suns,*
> *Her nostrils, deep and cavernous.*
>
> *Her ears stood like two thighs, straight up,*
> *Matted and twisted was Her hair;*
> *Her body was misshapen, huge,*
> *There was nothing that broke its height. (Stephen 166)*

With the beautiful Uma now transformed into the very likeness of Rangda, Siwa undergoes his own change taking on the form of the demonic god, Kala, who is likened to a roaring lion, which is one way one might describe the Barong mask. Quite unexpectedly, the divine pair, now as Durga and Kala, begin to destroy everything that Uma had created, most pointedly they begin to devour mankind. They might have succeeded in undoing everything had not other gods intervened. Stephen describes the resolution to the myth in the following:

The Litany of Resi Bhujangga reveals how humankind are saved from the depredations of Durga and Siwa/Kala. The High God sends Brahma, Wisnu, and Mahesvara down to earth. They become priests, one a Resi [ascetic], one a Brahmana Priest, and one a Bhujangga priest [artist]. Together they taught human beings how to make ritual offerings of food to the destroyers and their followers. When presented with their offerings, an astonishing transformation takes place in Siwa/Kala and Durga (Hooykaas 1974, 75):

> *Gone is the form that They then had,*
> *To Their first form They have returned;*
> *God Kala, Guru has become,*
> *And Durga, Uma has become.*

The gods of the four directions, who had previously been cursed to take demonic form, now revert to god form; Korsika becoming Iswara, Garga becoming Brahma, Maitri becoming Mahadewa, Kurusya becoming Wisnu and Pratanjala becoming Siwa. The demonic followers of Durga and Kala become heavenly musicians and nymphs. (173)

In both academic papers, Stephen links the Barong and Rangda encounter with other esoteric texts. The arrival on earth in demonic form by Uma and Siwa as Rangda and Barong is always the result of inappropriate lovemaking. In the *Kalatattwa*, Siwa sees the thigh of his wife, Uma, and though she resists his advances, he ejaculates. The sperm falls into the ocean, which began to churn violently eventually taking the form of Kala (but in the temple he will be called Durga). Those who break the laws, who do not perform sacrifices, become food for this demonic presence on earth. If people do perform the rituals correctly, then Kala/Durga may return to heaven in his peaceful form (*somyarupa*) (Stephen "Returning" 69). In another text, *Siwagama*, Siwa and Uma are not flying over the ocean when he is overcome with desire, but rather had descended to the east of Mount Meru. In this case Siwa actually forces Uma to have intercourse with him, whereupon she gives birth to the fearsome Kala. Unlike the *Kalatattwa* it is the High God who descends on earth taking on the form of a one-legged animal and then an old woman, which frustrate Kala to no end when he cannot catch them and devour them. Finally Kala kneels at the feet of the High God in the form of an old woman and begs forgiveness. The High God then instructs humans to worship the gods and ancestors or they will be devoured by Kala. Stephen summarizes the similarities and differences between the two texts, *Kalatattwa* and *Siwagama* in the following passage:

> We find that in these texts Kala begins as an uncontrolled power threatening to destroy everything in its path, although in one account he is said to be only searching for his parents. Finally, he is confronted by either *Sang Hyang Widi*, the high god, or his parents, Siwa and Uma, who bring him under control and give him both rights and duties to fulfil in the world. He is given the right to devour human beings who do not respect the laws of *dharma* and who fail to worship the ancestors and the gods. It is his duty to punish wrongdoers, but also to protect and give success to those who correctly perform the prescribed rituals and sacrifices. Furthermore, both texts explain that if these offerings are correctly made, Kala and his deputies will resume a gentle form (*somyarupa*), and return to Siwa's heaven. (71)

Thus, Stephen proposes that the course of the mythological narrative traces the path of the ritual in which the narrative is performed. The impure, polluted forms of Uma (Durga, Rangda, and a lowest form "Bhuta Dengen" (182)) are invoked one after the other becoming progressively more base and "lower" in the divine hierarchy. The narrative then mirrors the course and purpose of the ritual, which is to produce purity. Stephen writes:

> Although the variations tend to be confusing, the same basic principle is evident: there are infinite transformations of "mother power" involved, from the highest and most perfect, to the lowest and most terrible. These highest and lowest points are usually

represented in the forms of Uma and Rangda, but according to my informants there are both lower and higher points beyond these, so that Rangda's form gives way to even lower entities, such as Kalika and Bhuta Dengen, while Uma transforms upwards to Siwa, to Parama Siwa, and ultimately to the high god, Tunggal, the single perfect unity. There are often not one but two Rangda masks kept by the temple—one white, one red. The white mask represents the more positive form of Durga, the protector, the red mask represent (*sic.*) the more dangerous, angry form, Berawi. Thus the two masks depict a dual potential within Rangda herself. (182)

Stephen continues to discuss how *The Calon Arang* epic fits this very same mythological pattern for the narrative. Durga appears to the Widow of Girah who transforms into Rangda, a representation of "destructive power in its most virulent form" (183). Rangda is then cleansed by Mpu Baradah, who takes the form of the Barong, "redirecting that power in a positive direction" back toward Durga and ultimately Uma.

What becomes clear is that the story, unlike many of the early foreign interpretations, is not about good defeating evil, which remains the interpretation on brochures handed to tourists who attend a daily performance of the dance drama in Batu Bulan or Ubud. Even within the mythological and historical narratives, there are other stories simultaneously being told through the multivalent symbolism of the Barong and Rangda masks. Stephen details how a conversation with a mask maker, Ida Bagus Sutarja, led to his learning that the Barong, in addition to being associated with Mpu Baradah and with Siwa, is also symbolic of the sky, rain, semen, and the masculine principle:

His comical and flirtatious behavior takes on new meaning when we understand his role is in fact to woo Rangda. Rangda's element is fire, and her colour red, she symbolizes the earth, and the feminine principle... Her very name means "widow", that is to say she is a woman alone; cursed and rejected by her husband Siwa, her femine creative power thus turned destructive... In the meeting of fire and water, the fire is put out, the water disappears, and from this neutralizing (*dumulada*) of the two powers arises smoke or steam, which according to the esoteric teachings, represents the *atman* or soul (Suarka 1998)... The transformation of water and fire into steam symbolizes (or perhaps actually constitutes in a sense) the process of *nyomya*, returning to godlike form, since what arises out of that meeting is new life, or the *atman*. The material elements of fire and water are unified and dissolved to give rise to pure spirit. The angry mother goddess, symbolized by fire (womb, blood) and the sacred letter, ANG, is brought under control by water (the sacred letter AH), semen, from the creator god (see Suarka 1998, 7-8). (178-179)

The story of fire and water underlies the story not only of this ritual but of each individual human, whose cremation is performed as a "marriage between fire and water" (180), the fire burning the water in the body thereby releasing the steam and smoke (the soul, or *atman*) from earthly ties.

Along the lines of the individual, the encounter between Rangda and Barong also enacts a period of psychological development one inevitably faces in relation to their mothers. Here Stephen is able to incorporate some of the elements of the actual performance of the ritual that do not fit in neatly with either the narratives of either *The Calon Arang* epic or the Hindu myths detailed in *The Siwagama* or *The Kalatattwa*. At the height of the ritual, several men go into trance and are given sharp *krisses* with which to attack the trance dancer playing Rangda. Because the trance is real, the man playing Rangda is not wounded by the assaults, and the effect of their coming into contact with Rangda is that they turn their own *krisses* against themselves. This is interpreted by Stephen in the following way:

> One cannot destroy the angry mother. If you try to do so you only damage your self since your physical body and its components are derived from her. Rather she must be transformed by meeting with the Barong to bring her back to her more positive aspect. At this point the Barong re-enters and brings the kris dancers back to consciousness. Offerings are made and the Rangda is now taken back into the temple, along with the Barong and the kris dancers. (180)

# THE LAST CHAPTER

In the chapter at the end of this book, I will provide my own analysis of the performed encounters between Rangda and the Barong. My own analysis delves deeper into the past to a belief that may have existed prior to the introduction of Hinduism in Bali, to the indigenous belief that is common to most island cultures, *semangat* in Indonesia (*mana* in Hawaii). We have already seen many accounts of Rangda's appearance and how it is meant to represent the destructive, cursed form of Uma, which is in need of cleansing and purification. In my analysis I focus on how the iconography of the mask is meant to represent an expression and release of this life energy, which is believed to exist in all things to varying degrees. Something with a lot of semangat may be living or may be an inanimate object like a *kris*, which needs ritual attention to manage the presence of this energy. The energy is contained within, and, since women have the power to give life, they are considered to have more *semangat* than men. Tying one's hair in public, covering one's mouth when they smile, refraining from widening one's eyes in surprise are all cultural means of controlling this energy, and are behaviors expected of young girls and women by their parents and by society.

The energy is neither positive nor negative. It can be dangerous as well as nourishing, much like the ocean's ability to provide food for a village and then destroy it in a storm. In Rangda's case, she is a representation of unbridled power emanating from the masked dancer who is believed to be possessed by Rangda's spirit. Her required presence twice each year at a village cleansing ritual (*bersih desa*) is indicative of her beneficial role in not only guarding the village, but also cleansing it of black magic, disease, and crop failure. She truly is the heroine, not the villain, in the ritual performance of her mask, for it is her presence that causes the flow of *semangat* that refreshes what has turned stagnant, what has become polluted, what has been corrupted. One might imagine a flood of water clearing out a creek bed that has become clogged with garbage and debris.

The climax of the dance drama, in my interpretation, is not the encounter between the Barong and Rangda, but in the long interlude in which Rangda appears on the stage (*kalangan*) alone. As I discuss in the last chapter, her soliloquy breaks the boundaries of either the mythological or historical narrative as she directly challenges practitioners of black magic tormenting the village to turn their forces on her. If there is a blight affecting the rice, or an infestation of pests, she will command them to leave. While dangerous in the sense that nobody would want to make contact with Rangda while she is present on the stage, she has the interests of the village at heart, and anyone or anything that wants to harm the rice, the people, or the animals must go through her. The multi-layered stories (historical and mythological), then, provide a loose framework for Rangda to make her appearance. Her role in cleansing and purifying are paralleled by the ritual work done around the performance.

Offerings provide the means for physically cleansing a community. The work of preparing the offerings for the *bersih desa* or for any kind of cleansing ritual (referred to here generally as *selamatan*), as I argue elsewhere in the book *Setting a Plot*, inspires periods of intense productivity in which both men and women join together to assemble rice, fruits, flowers, and meat into ephemeral works of art (men assemble offerings of meat; women, of flowers, rice, and fruit). These are taken to the temple to be processed and blessed. They are dropped off in the outer courtyard where the performance is held, and various parts of the offering are removed by priests (such as money for the maintenance of the temple) when they are brought to the inner temple to be blessed. As I argue in the last chapter of this work, the offerings once played a more direct role in cleansing in that they were then placed outside the temple so that the poor, sick, and the needy could find nourishment. For many this was the only time they had access to meat.

Rangda's role in cleansing the village is paralleled by a male character, Sidha Karya, who is responsible for cleansing the entire island in a ritual known as Panca Wali Krama. After a bomb destroyed the Sari nightclub in October of 2002 killing hundreds of tourists and Indonesians alike, while the consul of Australia planned a memorial to those who had died on the site of the attack, the Balinese response was to hold a Panca Wali Krama ritual.

Those responsible for the bomb belonged to the extremist group Jemaah Islamiyah, which claims to be linked to Al Qeda. The bomb destroyed an entire block and blew a crater in the ground more than ten feet deep. Body parts were found on roof tops several blocks away. Panic set over the entire island of Bali immediately as tourists, who feared further attacks, swarmed the airport in an attempt to flee. Hotels were emptied. The thousands that were employed in the tourist industry would eventually lose their jobs, and, in addition to the miserable grief for those who lost their lives, an economic depression set in that Bali has never really completely recovered from.

Whereas The Calon Arang is designed to cleanse a village, the Panca Wali Krama ritual is aimed at cleansing the entire island. The only ritual that is broader in scope and scale than this one is *Eka Dasa Rudra*, which, held for several months only once every one hundred years, is devoted to cleansing the entire world. The masked character Sidha Karya and Rangda share many character-istics. Both feature long shocks of hair on the top, although Rang-da's mask also features locks of hair that trail down below the waist of the person who plays her. While generally Sidha Karya has narrow upturned eyes and the eyes of Rangda are bulging out of their sockets, both Sidha Karya and Rangda feature prominent tusks that protrude from their lips. Both are distinctly demonic in form; both seem to represent impure but powerful forms of their human counterparts, the "widow" of Girah and Ida Sangkhya respectively.

The stories associated with the masked characters both add elements of "foreignness" to the origins of these characters. In the case of Rangda, as mentioned by Curnow, the "widow" was banished from her position as queen to King Udayana for prac-ticing witchcraft. She writes: "In Bali and Java the mythic figure of Calon Arang has become entwined with historical fact: she is iden-tified with Mahendradatta, a Javanese princess who married the Balinese King Udayana, and is said to have practiced black magic, for which her husband exiled her to the forest" (32). At the begin-ning of Sidha Karya's story, an old man appears at the gates to the sixteenth century kingdom of Waturenggong. In some cases he is from Java, but there are versions that state he has traveled all the way from India to assist and guide the king, whom he claims to be related to, with a ritual that is taking place. In either case, the guards at the gate drive him away, assuming such a filthy, homeless mendicant couldn't possibly be related to the king.

Each case places the masked characters outside the domestic realm of the kingdom. The widow appears to have taken up residence in the village of Girah, which complicates her "foreign" identity, but the village is referred to as being on the outskirts of the kingdom, near its periphery. The widow is distinctly outside of the domestic bond of marriage, which is compounded by the problem that nobody will marry her daughter. The wandering mendicant, Ida Sangkhya, appears not only to be unmarried, but also poor and without a home.

In each case, the initial tension that is created by this lack of belonging to the domestic sphere of either the home or the kingdom is replaced with a greater, more pressing problem: that of impurity and pollution. Beaten and bruised, Ida Sangkhya wanders into the hills where his despair catches the attention of Dewa Gunung, or the God of the Mountain, who unleashes demons upon Waturenggong's kingdom just as the king was seeking to purify it with a grand ritual. The offerings begin to rot before they are even placed at the shrine, dancers begin to quarrel and argue, and finally an enormous demon arrives and destroys the mother temple, Besakih. In each case, the legend brings the realm to a point of terrible corruption and ruin. We may recall that the widow's witchcraft, spread by her disciples, causes death and disease in people, animals, and crops alike.

Elsewhere I have argued that domesticity is a central concern in the epics of river valley cultures such as Vedic India. The classic tale of a war fought to bring back an abducted wife is told in *The Ramayana* as well as *The Iliad and Odyssey*, "The Story of Dinah" in The Book of Genesis, and in several Chinese legends. In *Setting a Plot*, I argue that that in island cultures the problem of domestic/foreign boundaries is not nearly as urgent as the problem of pollution and the depletion of resources, which island cultures faced and overcame early in their histories or else went the way of Rapanui (Easter Island, which depleted the resources, suffered from famine, and nearly went extinct). Thus, in both of the Balinese dramas, *Sidha Karya* and *The Calon Arang*, the problems of domesticity and belonging, whether outside of bonds of marriage or the boundaries of the kingdom (foreign), are replaced with the much more immediate problem of pollution, recentering the tension around the opposition between polluted/pure rather than foreign/domestic.

Interestingly, the solution to restoring purity lies in the "foreign." The purity and productivity of Waturenggong's kingdom is only restored when he sends troops to find and bring Ida Sangkhya (the foreigner) back to the kingdom, where he is given a seat right next to the king for the remainder of the ritual dances and prayers. Ida Sangkhya is given the honor of making the final offering of the five-colored rice, which is thrown in the four cardinal directions (and the middle). Just prior to offering this special rice, Ida Sangkhya makes his transformation into his more powerful form as Sidha Karya, donning the mask with long hair and protruding teeth, as well as the gloves that make his fingernails appear six inches long.

Rangda and Sidha Karya's essential function as cleansers coupled with their demonic, *kasar* or unrefined appearances are an example of what Kodi et. al. refer to as *rwu bhineda*, which they translate as "two principles in opposition" (174-175). The two principles cannot be separated from one another:

> In this dichotomization of insider Balinese and outsider from over the seas, we see an interaction of the Balinese concept of *rwu bhineda*—two principles in opposition. The white and the black, the male and female, the mountain and the sea, the divine and demonic, life and death—dualities pervade Balinese thinking. You cannot have one thing without its opposite. As the land wells up out of the sea, so the ruler rises from the people, and so the divine rises from the ground of the demonic. Watu Renggong and Sidha

Karya are tied to each other, just as the Barong (the protective lion-like figure) and Rangda (the demonic widow-witch) are linked in The Calon Arang dance performance. Though the pairs seem in opposition, the narrative needs both parties to progress. This idea of power from outside that must be reconciled within the system is a through-line in Balinese performance. The refinement and the very life of the refined partner—here Watu Renggong—come in a mysterious way from the ground of the more distorted chthonic sibling—here Sidha Karya. The pairing reminds one, too, of the relationship of the child and his/her strongest spirit sibling, which in Balinese thought is represented by the afterbirth. Balinese revere and propitiate the dangerous other that is our source and succor.

In the version of *Sidha Karya* presented by I Ketut Kodi and his collaborators, the demonic is associated with outsiders. Kuta with its hedonistic Australian and American tourists, the immigration of Javanese Muslims workers-turned-terrorists, and even the seemingly intractable situation of local poverty—these three situations are all bundled with the Sidha Karya character. The disruptions these three problems represent to the elite and the powerful of Bali must be addressed to move forward. A society that does not find ways to incorporate the potentially disruptive in positive ways is vulnerable.

The Bali bomb, in the interpretation of these artists, was not just an outside attack on innocent victims in the way that the American 9/11 is represented in the U. S. media. Via the ideology of *rwu bhineda*, "us" cannot be separated from "them" in the simplistic dichotomies of American patriotic or Islamic fundamentalist rhetorics that revisit ideas of crusade or jihad of the monotheistic faiths from which they derive. In the Balinese conception "we" are "them"—Watu Renggong is the brother of Sidha Karya. (174-175)

The Balinese concept of *rwu bhineda* undoes the boundary between foreign and domestic in putting forth notions that there is no "us" without "them." I would argue that this should be applied to the opposition between demonic and divine as well. Very much in keeping with Michele Stephen's notions of a continuum between Uma, Durga, and Rangda, we see the tendency for the divine and the pure to become corrupted, polluted, and demonic only to be restored to their original forms. This philosophy is mirrored in the landscape of Bali as well, which does not feature such a rigid boundary between domestic crops and wild, untended forest. In Bali, the domesticated fields of rice are inundated with wild animals (eels, frogs, and small fish) as well as plants (especially algae) to temporarily produce something much more akin to a wild pond than a domesticated field. In his work *Priests and Programmers*, J. Stephen Lansing refers to the process underlying Bali's engineered landscapes as "artificial ecology" (38). The secret of Bali's success with rice was in recognizing the rejuvenating power of wild systems on domesticated land. Thus, the alignments between domestic/foreign and domestic/wild are intentionally undone in order to restore the balance between the most essential binary opposition: that of purity and pollution. For an island people, their very existence depends on constantly renewing the same land one has used for more than two millennia. Productivity depends on purity, and purity is only accomplished with the undoing of boundaries rather than their rigid maintenance and establishment.

Therefore, Rangda's destructive, unrefined, polluted presence at the center of the purification ritual, like that of Sidha Karya's, becomes not only expected but required if the result of the cere-mony is to be productive purity. The creative and rejuvenating powers of what is wild and undomesticated within its opposition to what is domestic is aligned with and ultimately informs the other oppositions between domestic and foreign as well as divine and demonic. Rather than seeing purification as an attempt to dismiss or drive away the impure, demonic, corrupted, and polluted, the Balinese attempt to bring those very undesirable qualities right into the center where ritual activity may break them down and recombine them into the pure, creative qualities associated with Siwa and Uma.

# A "WHITE" TELLING OF A "BROWN" STORY

In the third volume of the *Live to Tell* series on storytelling, currently forthcoming with Wayzgoose Press, I discuss my concerns, my awareness of criticisms, my reservations, and yet my persistence in telling stories from the canon of Balinese folklore. In that volume, I am most interested in the interface between traditional folklore and personal storytelling, but I go into depth about cultural appropriation, or more aptly, cultural misappropriation. My linking a personal story to the grand epic of *The Calon Arang* certainly raises these very same questions, to which there may not be a definite answer.

First of all, I assume that I am writing for a mainly white, or at least Western audience. I no longer pretend that my audience is universal, and to do so is to perpetuate the very myths of universality and individualism that are underpinnings of white privilege both in the United States and globally. Robin DiAngelo's book *White Fragility* has done much to increase my awareness of how the accusation that I am appropriating Balinese culture might produce knee-jerk defensiveness in me as a white storyteller. I suppose one possible course of action would have been for me to stop telling Balinese folk tales because I am not Balinese, and I have not received explicit permission to tell stories such as *The Calon Arang*. Even if I received permission from one person, such as the priests or temple dancers I interviewed in producing the third chapter of this work, that might still not provide me with adequate license to tell this story without the implication that I am appropriating (or misappropriating) this grand narrative.

My tendency over the years as I have become increasingly aware of my own privilege has been to withdraw further and further into scholarship and academia as I present the stories, which is again an attempt to root myself in "objectivity and universality," the classic places of retreat for white privilege. Indeed, I have benefited from a system that allowed me, a twenty-year-old white American with few skills whatsoever, to go to Bali as a volunteer "to help" Balinese society. I went to teach English, but while I was a native speaker, I had no formal training as a teacher. In reality, of course, I received much more from Bali than I was ever able to give the Balinese. The whole volunteer program was, now that I think about it, actually aimed at benefiting me, providing me with a meaningful and enriching experience, and not the people in the Asian countries to which the program was paying lip service.

My stubborn-ness in persisting with my telling of this epic, framed within my own personal narrative, is because I believe that there actually is something universal about this format for telling the story—certainly closer to universal than telling either the epic on its own, or my personal tale on its own—and that is the spark that is created by the epic in the person who hears the story to tell a story of their own. The capacity for traditional tales to inspire a listener to tell their own story, to fit themselves into the narrative, and to explore how the age old narrative relates to themselves and the problems they are facing is, I am beginning to believe more and more, the most universal aspect of storytelling. In an age when personal stories are diverging more and more widely from traditional stories, I hope to highlight the power of connecting personal stories with folklore.

My personal tales are rooted in true experiences that occurred in the early 90s when I was living on the outskirts of the village of Tonja. My meeting with Rangda as she sprinted down the road toward the city of Denpasar was something that I will never forget, and it certainly fired my imagination. I suppose to me, this experience was an indication of the degree to which I would have to be open to what could possibly happen in a given moment while living in Bali, and it fits in with many other stories I tell about my life there, where wild and strange things happen on bus rides, in one's own home late at night, or at wedding ceremonies. To me, Bali is a romantic, magical place where I met the woman I am spending my life with and where I hope to return to spend my final days. This is not what Bali is like to a Balinese person.

*The Calon Arang* has also inspired modern Indonesian storytellers and writers. I have already mentioned Pramoedya Ananta Toer's retelling of the epic in Indonesian prose, securing the epic's place today in Indonesia as one of the most popular and widely known sagas of ancient literature. This is not to mention that Rangda continues to appear in village rituals regularly, invoked as the guardian and protectress of each village approximately twice a year. Tourists and Indonesians alike wear shirts that bear both her image and that of the Barong.

In addition, modern authors including Goenawan Mohamad, Toeti Heraty, and Cok Sawitri have recreated scenes from *The Calon Arang* to varying degrees. As I will discuss at the end of this book, these authors were moved to tell their own versions of Rangda's story. Their tellings form an important difference with mine in that they treat her epic background as fluid and open to question, whereas it is a static, fixed narrative for me. Their inspiration leads to the agency with which they respond to how Rangda has been mistreated, abused, and slandered by the respective powers of the state and the patriarchal tendencies of Indonesian and global society. My own story, in all of its shortcomings, can at least serve as a case with which to study the difference between an Indonesian story told by a white, western teller versus when it is in the hands of someone from that culture.

By comparison my retelling of *The Calon Arang* is far less significant politically and socially. Rangda provided the Indonesian writers with an opportunity to contest and question the authority that the state or even the village has had over her, and thereby invite the audience to completely reconsider the plot of the epic itself, recasting Rangda as a victim and heroine rather than villain and perpetrator. In their retellings, what scholars treat as a misunderstanding of her nature, these authors treat as an indictment of power, and an urgent plea to absolve Rangda of her demonization and stigmatization and reclaim her role as a nurturing, creative force.

The version of *The Calon Arang* that I wrote for the second chapter of this book is a simplified one based on a ritual performance of the story rather than on manuscripts or written works. I attended many village cleansing ceremonies after I was captivated by one early in my experience living in Bali. The rituals didn't always tell the complete story, and certainly did not appear to end with the Barong purifying Rangda before sending her back to heaven, which is the conclusion reached in written texts. In one version, which is discussed in the last chapter, the Barong collapsed during the performance and did not return, which leaves their encounter at the very least open-ended and possibly with the opposite outcome of the written manuscripts (Rangda apparently defeating the Barong!). All of the rituals featured men who attacked Rangda with *krisses* and then fell into trance, ultimately turning the *krisses* on themselves in an act known as *ngurek*. Therefore, I relate a looser, more open-ended denouement that features the Barong and Rangda retreating together and disappearing into the ocean, which is a casual version I heard numerous times from my students at Universitas Mahasaraswati and from people living in Canggu, where I also witnessed several performances.

While the withdrawal to the ocean may sound absurd at first, it is actually quite logical to associate Rangda, the cleanser, with the ocean, the ultimate point to which the water of the rice fields and villages carries waste and burnt remnants of the offerings. Lansing has written about the dual quality of water, especially holy water, *tirta*, whose upstream quality of purity (as it arrives to nourish a rice field) is paired with the downstream quality of pollution (as it bears away the waste and burnt trash from the field and village) (Lansing 54). The upstream quality is directed to Lake Batur, traditionally considered the source of all freshwater on the island. The goddess Dewi Danau resides there, and her purity is linked with the fertility and productivity of the island through her association with Dewi Sri, the Rice Goddess. They are both represented with the same motif, the *cili*, in offerings, and their shrines both appear at the upstream end of rice fields and irrigation groups known as *subak*. Both are refined and gentle in comparison to Rangda's coarse, fearsome energy. Thus Rangda's ultimate arrival in the ocean is reflective of both the physical ability of downstream water to bear away the impurities that are produced during everyday life, ultimately depositing them in the ocean, and her role in village cleansing ceremonies as the one who rids the village of spiritual corruption, depression, infestation, disease, and crop failure.

For me, Rangda was also a gatekeeper into Bali. My story captures the loneliness of the life I led before I met the sister and brother who would share my house with me for the next several years. In some ways, Rangda brought the village where I was living to me, physically leading the congregation, including the two siblings, into the garden of the home I was renting. In this way, Rangda's role as the interface between domestic and foreign, which was discussed earlier, was brought into play. She was constantly transgressing the barriers of temple and village, of sacred and profane, of public and private, as well as the significant one for me, which was the barrier between myself as a foreigner and the domestic space of the village.

My inclusion of my personal tales as frames around the traditional folklore of Rangda should serve, in addition to dramatizing Rangda's role in breaking and reforming boundaries, to illustrate how I locate and limit myself as a western teller against the rich folklore of Bali. I was truly frightened to death by the events in the tale itself, and I remain continually in awe of the complexity that Rangda represents to different people in Balinese society. I am constantly surprised and gratified to learn more about Rangda and to see whole dimensions of her identity that I may never be able to comprehend. If anything, I hope that my framing of the story of Rangda with my own anecdotes pushes my rendition as far as possible away from *appropriation* and toward the best possible outcome in this exchange, which is *appreciation*. This is truly my intention.

# WORKS CITED

- Curnow, Heather M. "Women on the Margins: An Alternative to Kodrat?" Doctoral Dissertation. Tasmania: Hobart School of Asian Languages and Studies, October 2007.
- Kodi, I. Ketut, I Gusti Putu Sudarta, I Nyoman Sedana, and Kathy Foley. "'Topeng' Sidha Karya: A Balinese Masked Dance." *Asian Theater Journal.* Vol. 22, No. 2. University of Hawaii Press. Autumn, 2005.
- Lansing, J. Stephen. *Priests and Programmers: Technologies of Power in the Engineered Landscape of Bali.* United States of America: Princeton University Press, 2007.
- Spies, Walter and Beryl de Zoete. *Dance and Drama in Bali.* London: Faber and Faber Limited, 1938.
- Stephen, Michele. "Barong and Rangda in the Context of Balinese Religion." *RIMA: Review of Indonesian and Malaysian Affairs.* Vol. 35, No. 1, Winter, 2001: 137-193.
- ----------. "Returning to Original Form: A Central Dynamic in Balinese Ritual." *Bijdragen tot de Taal—, Land— en Volkenkunde.* Vol. 158, No. 1. 2002: pp. 61-94.

- Suastika, I Made. *Calon Arang dalam Tradisi Bali.* Yogyakarta: Duta Wacana University Press, 1997.
- Toer, Pramoedya Ananta. *The King, the Witch, and the Priest.* Translated by William Samuels. 2002: Equinox Publishing, Singapore.

# PART II

TALES OF RANGDA

# THE TALES

*The street was quiet and all but abandoned for most of the journey, but at least a dozen neighborhood dogs would be waiting for me as I arrived at the Tonja Intersection.*

It was 11:30 pm, and I was pedaling home on my bicycle. I lived in a modest house of unplastered bricks on Jalan Nangka outside of Denpasar, Bali, Indonesia. It was about five kilometers outside the city of Denpasar. The house is still there, but whereas the house used to be in the middle of rice fields, now it is surrounded by enormous warehouses.

Every day around four in the afternoon, I would descend into the city with a bicycle that the landlord lent me. Classes at the college were from five in the evening to ten thirty at night. I taught English.

Coming down on the busy street in daylight was fine, but going home in the darkness was a different matter. Before making the bike ride home, I would cross the street to the night market and eat fried rice with my students. Then they would help me as I gathered ammunition. Most teachers kept papers in their briefcase, but I kept rocks! The street was quiet and all but abandoned for most of the journey, but at least a dozen neighborhood dogs would be waiting for me as I arrived at the Tonja Intersection.

As I neared the intersection, I would build up momentum, then throw my legs up on the handlebars. Coasting through, I would unload the rocks into the snouts of the dogs. There were snarls, and there were yelps of pain. Twice my pants were ripped; once, I needed stitches.

*Then I stopped. In the pale, blue moonlight I saw something large in the middle of the road.*

One night on a full moon, I expected a terrible fight with the dogs... but, as I neared the intersection, to my surprise, there were none. I coasted through... I even did a victory lap in the middle of the intersection... Why weren't there any dogs?

On the other side of the intersection, I began the slog up the hill toward Gang Dewi Sita. Then I stopped. In the pale, blue moonlight I saw something large in the middle of the road. It was moving fast from side to side. A large dog, I thought. Then it stopped, and reared up on its hind legs. It was enormous, much bigger than a dog.

I remained frozen as whatever it was seemed to study me from a hundred feet away... then it rushed toward me with surprising speed... I turned my bike around to head back downtown, but it had already arrived within a yard of me. It stopped. I held my breath. It raised an enormous claw against the luminescence of the night sky. I could hear my heart pounding in my ears. Then, whatever it was, let out a blood curdling howl. All of my hair stood on end... I felt faint.

Lights bobbed around me, and I thought I was losing consciousness. There were people in brightly colored clothing holding my arms and gently leading me to the side of the road. A ritual, The Calon Arang, was being moved from its place in the Pura Dalem, to this crossroads. The thing with claws was the Goddess, Rangda. A man wearing the horrifying white, fanged mask was supposedly possessed by the Goddess herself. In this appearance she had been displeased with her congregation and stormed out of the temple. She had sprinted down the street, and now the people were just catching up to her. Traffic was stopped in all directions. Priests laid offerings right in the middle of the intersection. The gamelan struck up. Then the Barong, a mythical dragon-like creature played by two people, arrived, and the ritual continued.

Exhausted and still trembling, I headed home.

*All the young men in the village, while they found Ratna Manggali to be quite beautiful, feared the widow, for they suspected, rightly, she was a powerful practitioner of black magic.*

The next day, I asked some of my students about the ritual, and about Rangda. They told me the legend behind this goddess that was acted out regularly in temples by members of the congregation wearing masks.

In the beginning of the eleventh century in East Java, there arose a perfect kingdom. Their king, Erlangga, fostered the arts and learning, and writing was brought to Indonesia taking the form of the lontar poetry and chronicles. One of the greatest of these chronicles is written about this very king and his kingdom. It is known as *The Calon Arang.*

From the fields fat cattle, sleek buffaloes, and rice bending under the weight of the ripening grain were regular sights, and from every hut came the sounds of laughter and the warm chatter of families. There was no poverty nor disease, and everyone in the kingdom was happy... all except for one person in the outlying village of Girah. It was a widow, known as Walu Nateng Dirah, whose main concern was finding an adequate match for her beautiful daughter, Ratna Manggali. All the young men in the village, while they found Ratna Manggali to be quite beautiful, feared the widow, for they suspected, rightly, she was a powerful practitioner of black magic.

Indignant, Walu Nateng Dirah demanded that the king himself, Erlangga, marry her daughter, but the king refused. This rejection started off a series of terrible events that nearly brought ruin to the great kingdom. At midnight the widow summoned her helpers, known as *sisya*, who gathered around her to receive their instructions.

In high-pitched eerie chanting, Walu Nateng Dirah ordered them to "take what was happy, healthy, and prosperous, and replace it with misery, disease, and poverty."

They shrieked, "We will take what is happy, healthy, and prosperous, and replace it with misery, disease, and poverty."

"Now go," Walu Nateng Dirah growled. "And spread death to all corners of the kingdom!"

*The rice began to wither in the fields. The skin began to hang off the gaunt frames of the cattle and buffalo. People became mysteriously ill. The laughter and warm chatter gave way to tears.*

The effects were immediate. The rice began to wither in the fields. The skin began to hang off the gaunt frames of the cattle and buffalo. People became mysteriously ill. The laughter and warm chatter gave way to tears.

King Erlangga met with his advisors to see what could be done. They recommended that he summon a great sage from the forest, whose name was Mpu Baradah. He lived in the woods, practicing meditation and yoga. Mpu Baradah could sit so still that ants would build their nests over his body. He could meditate with such focus that he might cause trees to burst into blossom, rivers and creeks to boil and bubble.

Meanwhile Walu Nateng Dirah continued to send her sisya out, and things only became worse in Erlangga's realm.

*As he walked further away from the realm toward Girah, the scenery became more and more depressing, then hopeless, and finally horrific.*

At the king's request, Mpu Baradah made the journey out to Girah to face the witch. As he walked further away from the realm toward Girah, the scenery became more and more depressing, then hopeless, and finally horrific. He passed rotting rice fields like black, fetid cesspool, then a dead buffalo that was so swollen with the gasses of decomposition that it looked like an elephant carcass, and then, to his horror, in the middle of the road, Mpu Baradah found the tiny corpse of a baby, half eaten by dogs.

The ground became black and oily, and the sickeningly sweet stench of death filled his nostrils. Flies buzzed everywhere. Mpu Baradah knew he was close.

A small hut stood surrounded by scorched ground. Mpu Baradah sensed that the witch was inside.

"Come out, Walu Nateng Dirah" he challenged, but the hut remained eerily silent.

"I know you have taken the prosperity of these people, and replaced it with poverty." But the hut remained silent.

"I know you have taken the health of these people and replaced it with disease." But still the hut remained silent.

"I know you have taken the happiness of this entire kingdom and replaced it with despair and hopelessness." Still silence.

What Mpu Baradah didn't know was that inside the hut, a transformation was taking place. Walu Nateng Dirah was summoning all of her powers.

*The door to the hut opened, and a clawed hand held the door frame.*
*Behind the claw, glowing eyes were visible.*

The door to the hut opened, and a clawed hand held the door frame. Behind the claw, glowing eyes were visible. Her swollen tongue was bursting through her lips and hung down to her waist. Flames of enchantment flickered from her eyes, her nose, and the corners of her mouth. In one hand she held a white piece of cloth on which she had written powerful mantras of black magic. She lurched forward toward the sage.

Mpu Baradah unsheathed his keris and flew at her. He drilled the sacred weapon into her bristling body.

The Calon Arang didn't resist his assault in the slightest. Remaining completely limp in his grasp, she effortlessly repelled the blade.

Weakened by his contact, the sage withdrew. The Calon Arang seemed to be invulnerable. She gave a piercing shriek of triumph.

*The two began to fight. Fire flew in every direction. They chased each other, grappled, and threw one another.*

Mpu Baradah quickly slipped into a deep meditation to summon all of his powers, and then he too began to transform. He took the form of a never before seen dragon, with a red face, enormous, bulging, bright eyes, and a long, square, black beard.

The two began to fight. Fire flew in every direction. They chased each other, grappled, and threw one another.

Their fighting took them out of the kingdom to the coast of East Java. They fought in the water through the strait and arrived on the beaches of Bali. They fought around the north coast and down the east coast.The Calon Arang dropped her cloth on the beach of what is today Sanur. Today, the most powerful practitioner of black magic in all of Southeast Asia is rumored to live somewhere in Sanur and own that scarf, but nobody knows who it is. The two continued their raging battle on Sanur Beach into the surf and under the water facing Nusa Penida where it is said they continue their eternal battle to this very day.

*There was an eerie silence. I reached for the door handle.*

I fell asleep one night thinking of this story. I was awakened by a horrible sound. Had I been dreaming? I sprang from my bed.

My house had a covered porch with several rooms. Since I was the only one living there, I used one as an office, but the others were empty. As I went out onto the porch, to my horror, the door of one of the empty rooms was slowly closing. It shut with a click. Whatever it was was in the bedroom. I stood just outside the door. I could sense something just on the other side of the door.

My landlord had hoped that when he leased the house to me for two years, that I would pay for the finishing work on the house to be done. It needed plaster, and windows. It had a roof but it needed indoor ceilings put in. But I was a volunteer English teacher living on about a hundred dollars a month. I had windows put in, and, to keep the bats from flying around my head as I slept, I paid to have a bamboo ceiling to shut my bedroom off from the rafters. But the house remained unplastered brick walls with a very rough concrete floor. It had become a bone of contention between me and the landlord, and then there was the subject of blessing the house (*melaspas*), which would require an expensive ritual, something that he hoped I would pay for as well.

My students were always asking me if I was afraid to live alone in a house with so many empty rooms. The fact that the house wasn't even finished made it more serious in their minds. I had even asked some of them if they wanted to take one of the bedrooms for free, but none of them did. I think they were afraid.

"Hello," I called through the door. "Is somebody there?"

There was an eerie silence. I reached for the door handle. Before I could turn it, there was a bang on the other side of the door, and I fell over backward in fright. An inhuman howl seemed to be coming not from just the bedroom, but from the entire house! I stumbled out into the garden near the gate. It was the middle of the night, and I had to get help.

I made my way up the slippery mud path to Jalan Nangka, and there, to my surprise, a large crowd was gathered. People rushed to my side, and within moments the entire village in their temple finest were filing down Gang Dewi Sita into my garden. Once again, Rangda had fled from the temple. Moving faster than any of the priests or congregation members, they had not seen where she had gone.

Priests laid offerings by the door to the empty bedroom. The gamelan had been brought into the garden, which was now completely packed with men and women. Cigarette smoke mingled with the sweet incense, and there was laughter and lively chatter. I saw my landlord, who was mortified. We had to finish the house; we had to have the cleansing ceremony; we would talk later.

*Priests gathered on both sides of her as she stood in front of her congregation.*

Suddenly, there was a hush. The door was opening. Long finger-nails, trembling with energy appeared. There was a gasp from the congregation, and they all knelt respectfully.

From the darkness of the bedroom, a white face appeared. It was the mask of Rangda, but it seemed to be shimmering with life, like the man playing the mask had been bonded to it by the spirit of the Goddess. She slowly emerged. Priests gathered on both sides of her as she stood in front of her congregation.

There was a long moment of silence as she seemed to be looking at each person. She ran the white cloth she carried in one hand through the long claws of the other.

She raised her empty hand above her head, and then waved it in a downward motion as if dismissing everyone. "Eeeeeaaaaaaaaahhh-hhhhhh." That had been the same howl that had awakened me about an hour earlier.

Without warning, she jumped off the porch and went chugging through the crowd, which parted for her. One poor young man tried to squeeze in with the people on the right, but there was no room. He was moving to the other side when Rangda plowed right into him. Rangda's progress wasn't hindered a bit. She seemed to run right through him.

Actually, she had knocked him a considerable distance into a rice paddy. The poor young man was covered with mud. He tried to light a cigarette, but his matches were too wet and muddy.

Everyone began filing out of the garden. The gamelan was removed. All that was left was the lingering smoke of incense, and the young man. His sister also stayed to help him clean up.

I eventually came to a compromise with the landlord. I paid for the house to be finished, and he paid for the House Blessing Cere-mony. It was fascinating to be at the center of a ritual. Priests moved with holy water around the entire boundary of the property. There were many, many offerings heaped in piles around the garden and inside the house. The landlord's family and many of the villagers came to pray there. The stones and wood and bricks and plaster were symbolically reincarnated into their natural, living states and then unified into a whole that was this house.

Maybe the best thing to come out of this was the fact that I got two young people to live with me. It was the young man who had been plowed by Rangda, and, of course, his sister. Over the months and then the years, they taught me so much about Bali and Indonesia. I learned to speak Indonesian from them, and we became like a little family.

Now, as I live in the United States, I often think of them. I miss them, and I miss Bali.

# PART III

## RITUAL PERFORMANCES OF RANGDA

# INTRODUCTION: THE "PLAY" WITHIN
# THE PLAY

This chapter examines how print and print culture have changed ritual in Bali. The dissemination of printed texts and the growth of literacy have transformed and reshaped the way ritual is performed. While print has provided new media for the preservation and transmission of knowledge, many of the orally oriented methods of production and consumption have persisted within the literate societies of Indonesia, if only in Indonesia's rural margins. Television, theater productions, novels—all print-based media—have not displaced ritual in Bali. They have, however, had an effect on the modes by which ritual is produced and consumed.

This discussion will analyze dramatic rituals, examining the modern print conventions embraced by Indonesia's stability-promoting New Order government from the very late 1960s to 1998. These conventions, which separate the audience from the performance, have in profound ways altered the form of Indonesian ritual. The audience in Bali was traditionally interactive. Indonesia's appropriation of print media has resulted most notably in much more passive audiences, who cast themselves as spectators, not participants. A trend in scholarship points out how ritual has been "rationalized," and the chaos that erupted has been suppressed. But Indonesia's political and cultural absorption of print media has not been as sweeping as some scholars claim. While this scholarship is astute and helpful in illuminating how ritual was re-aligned with New Order ideology, it perceives the surface and overlooks the subtext. For the chaos of has been buried but not eradicated. At significant moments during the ritual, the audience surges onto the stage area to engage in a very participatory and physical interaction with the performers.

## Ritual Drama and Rhetorical Contracts

Richard Schechner has contributed valuable characterizations of many genres of theater, ritual drama among them. His collaborations with Victor Turner have introduced the interface between ritual and theater as a fruitful topic of anthropological research and speculation (Turner 80-93). Schechner posits ritual drama as one pole in an opposition he perceives as crucial to understanding world drama. The Greek theater, as Schechner discusses, evolved out of competitions. In these competitions, plays were performed before a panel of judges. Originally, awards were presented only to the authors of the winning plays. Out of such events, two characteristics of Greek drama have persisted, shaping Western drama for more than two thousand years. First, and most relevant to this discussion, is the separation of the performer from the audience. Originally composed of a panel of judges, the audience was completely removed, observing the drama and evaluating its merit. The fact that these original audiences were judges, not spectators, drives a wedge between the performers and the audience, for judges, in order to be objective, must be detached. The emotional detachment required of the judge/ audience has become a literal and physical barrier manifested in the structure of theaters themselves, specifically the impermeable boundary between the stage and the seated audience. Second is the emphasis on the text. It is the author who was awarded in the original competitions, not the actors. Such a construct prioritizes the writer and the written word. Performers are then merely the means of expression. In this paper, I will refer to these two qualities of Greek theater, the metaphorical and literal barrier between the audience and the performers, and the emphasis on the writer over the performers, as the "print-oriented contract" between performance and audience.

In contrast to this Western focus on the writer, Indian ritual drama, according to Schechner, is characterized by *'rasa'* ('flavor' or 'taste'), which he describes as "the mutuality, the sharing, the co-creation of preparers and partakers" (Schechner 140). Thus, Indian ritual drama overturns and counteracts the two qualities of print-oriented drama discussed above. "Mutuality" does away with the barrier print-oriented drama enforces between the performance and the audience. "Co-creation" suggests that not only do the performers in the drama "create" the text they interpret, but also the audience contributes to this act of creation. Thus, the print-oriented construct of the author as sole agent and creator does not exist in Indian ritual drama. Rather than separation between the performers and the audience, there is unity. The ritual drama involves the audience, who participates rather than evaluates.

The same word, "*rasa,*" is found in the Indonesian language, and also means "taste." The word bears many subtle meanings within the realms of mysticism and letters. Clifford Geertz has analyzed the concept of *rasa* within Javanese belief. Geertz translates the word as both "feeling" and "meaning" (Geertz *Religion* 238). This dual meaning, according to Geertz, illuminates a central tenet of Javanese mysticism: the unity of feeling and meaning, and the tight association of subjective experience with truth (see Hadiwijono 128). Within the realm of Indonesian composition and performance, *rasa* is a major element. As pointed out by I Kuntara

Wiryamartana in his analysis of the manuscript *Arjunawiwaha, rasa* is the overlying tone which creates unity throughout the poem's thousands of verses (Wiryamartana 346).

For the purposes of this discussion, I will use Schechner's definition of *rasa* as mutuality, since Schechner's scholarship specifically addresses ritual drama. In order to understand the mutuality endemic to Balinese ritual drama, it is useful to briefly consider Margaret Mead and Gregory Bateson's film *Trance and Dance in Bali* (1938). This film presented a Balinese ritual drama in which men and women stabbed themselves with *krisses*, a process known as *ngurek*. Much has been written about the making of this film. Of central concern to scholars is the fact that the film featured young women going into trance, instead of older women who normally performed this role in temple rituals. These young women were trained exclusively for the film. Because of this bizarre substitution, the authenticity of the film has recently been discredited (Pollman 27). To suit the medium of film, the production of the ritual drama was oriented to an audience that was consuming the film visually. This audience is the passive, spectating, print-oriented audience established by Greek drama. The substitution of young women for the old, undoubtedly designed to reinforce an image of Bali as exotic and beautiful, indicates that Bateson and Mead's projected audience is a foreign one, and one that follows the dictates of print-oriented conventions. It is an audience that watches.

What was noticeably absent in Mead and Bateson's film was the audience for which such a ritual drama is presented: the temple community or congregation. In the film, the interaction between the performers and the congregation was not represented, except during one incident. When the young women pressed the *krisses* against their breasts, an older woman rushed from the off-stage space behind the camera to join them. The camera followed the old woman as she took a *kris* and joined the *ngurek*. The old woman became a central part of the performance, in spite of Mead's efforts to produce a scene in which only beautiful, young women sway with their hair loosened in the dense incense smoke.

The frame of Margaret Mead's camera formed a stage out of the open temple courtyard, forcing the conventions of print on ritual drama. The film seldom gives the impression that there was an audience present during the performance except for that instant when the old woman marched from the off-screen space to join the young women in trance. Her intrusion marks a break in the seamlessness of the filmed drama, requiring explanation from Margaret Mead. Mead copes with this intervention by subtly chastising the old woman for breaking the rules of print-oriented drama, rules which require the audience to stay off-stage, off-camera: Mead complains, "[she] said she wouldn't go into trance." Simultaneously, though, Mead tries to smooth over this rupture in her carefully orchestrated staging, her substituting of old women with the more camera-friendly lovely young women her foreign audiences expect, by casting the old woman as a performer. She may be a performer who has disobeyed the rules, but Mead never acknowledges her as a wayward member of the audience, one who refused to stay in place. Schechner, who makes mention of this film in his book, points out that in one of Margaret Mead's talks it was revealed that those involved in the production of the film had been angered by the old woman's intrusion, for "... her trance had disturbed the aesthetic refinements they had rehearsed for foreign eyes—and foreign lenses'" (Schechner 75).

The old woman's intrusion into the frame of the camera reveals two different conceptions of the performance, the print-oriented one and the ritual one. Those who had choreographed the performance with Mead and Bateson quite clearly had the frame of the camera in mind, making these "aesthetic refinements" for their audience who would view the performance on the screen. For the old woman, however, there was no such separation between the performance and the audience. She played a participatory role in the production of the drama rather than a passive, observing, evaluating role.

My discussion of Margaret Mead's film has introduced the two different modes of orientation—that of the passive viewer, and that of the active, creative participant. Bali has to a degree changed its delineation of the role of the audience, in accommodation to print-oriented consumption. Performances which are intended as artistic as opposed to religious, in other words, performances presented before urban audiences, frequently paying audiences which include tourists, followed the print contract much more consistently and obediently. The audience stayed in their seats. Rural ritual dramas contain a mix of the two competing and contradictory traditions: at set times, the stage was as impermeable as any stage of a Greek drama, and the audience passively consumed. But at critical junctures, for reasons I will discuss, this contract, like the boundaries of the stage, gave way, and the audience members flooded on-stage to participate in the performances they had been quietly watching.

## Modernization, Rationalization, and Legitimization

Much has been written about the impact of modernity on what may very loosely be referred to as "Balinese culture." Clifford Geertz, in his essay "'Internal Conversion' in Contemporary Bali" and Anthony Forge, in his article "Balinese Religion and Indonesian Identity" both observe and examine the process of "rationalization" of Balinese culture and, in particular, of religion. For Clifford Geertz, "rationalization" occurs via "internal conversion," leading Balinese to self-consciously examine their religion, Bali-Hindu, in relation to Islam and Christianity. Forge's article characterizes the transformation he observes as defensive, and reactive to the national government's dismissive regard of Bali-Hindu. His article points out that shortly after Indonesian independence when the Ministry of Religion was founded, only Islam and Christianity were recognized as official religions of Indonesia. Forge argues that Bali has established its own Ministry of Religion in an attempt to dispel notions that the Bali-Hindu religion is a "religion of ignorance" and to present the Bali-Hindu religion in a rationalized manner to the National Ministry in Jakarta. In order to dispel such notions, Bali-Hindu needed to create and present texts. In other words, Bali-Hindu had to re-invent itself through print, from oral to literate. The underlying vehicle to both Geertz's notion of rationalization, and Forge's notion of legitimization, then, is the printed text.

The easy substitution of "rationalization" for "modernization" made by both Geertz and Forge suggest that this process of change is actually a process of removing what is "irrational" in the Balinese culture. John Pemberton has explored a similar issue in his book *On the Subject of 'Java'* which examines the devaluation and suppression of aspects of Javanese ritual that conflict with the rational, "modern" image of Indonesia promoted by the New Order government. All three writers make it perfectly clear why this "rationalizing" is occurring. Geertz describes a new Balinese society, particularly located in the educated youth of that society, beginning to question themselves and their own religion, thereby generating a new level of self-awareness and abstraction. Forge makes it clear that the Balinese, through the establishment of local government institutions such as the Balinese Ministry of Religion, seek legitimacy for the Bali-Hindu religion. Pemberton suggests that the suppressions he observed in Java are in keeping with the New Order's commitment to public security and national stability.

By analyzing the role that print plays in the ritual sphere I hope to clarify one mode by which "rationalization" and "modernization" occur. While Pemberton argues that chaos and disorder have successfully been suppressed in ritual, the observations I made while filming village cleansing rituals in Bali lead me to believe otherwise. The conditions under which rituals are performed today in Bali are much more conflicted. There is definitely a pull towards a more "ordered" version of the ritual, as Pemberton believes, but co-existent with this is an active resistance to such change.

In this chapter, I will briefly describe three rituals that I filmed while I was on a Humanities Research Grant in Bali from June until August, 1995. Two of the rituals presented a Calon Arang drama, while the third featured a Barong drama. At the climax of these dramas, the *kris* dancers, who are often thought to be the followers of the Barong, attack Rangda, drilling their sharp weapons into the body of the Rangda performer. The people attending the rituals that I filmed rose to their feet and poured onto the stage, creating the chaos that Pemberton asserts as being suppressed in the Javanese rituals he examined.

While my observations seem to contradict Pemberton's assertions, they actually contribute to a more diverse picture of Indonesian ritual. Pemberton witnessed very prominent rituals performed in urban arenas. These rituals involved officials from the national government and were large events worthy of coverage by the press. Significantly, Pemberton makes use of the news coverage of the ritual, rather than the ritual itself, in order to describe the ritual's suppression of chaos and disorder and thereby make his point. It is hardly surprising that such mediated representations of the ritual, in print no less, describe the ritual as conforming to the print contract.

"Chaos" has only become acknowledged as such with the introduction of print into Indonesian society. In order to appreciate such a statement, "chaos" must be understood to refer specifically to the audience's intrusion upon the stage. The congregation's entrance upon the stage has undoubtedly continued with predictable regularity at certain moments during Balinese ritual dramas for centuries, and is hardly wild, dangerous, and unpredictable as the term "chaos" seems to suggest. Thus, "chaos" once fit within the protocol of ritual drama, was expected, traditional, a following of rules instead of defiance of them. This flow of the audience upon the stage only becomes an unruly violation within the protocol of a print-oriented performance. When one expects the audience to remain seated and separate from the performance, such movements on their part suddenly become an infringement upon the boundary that is so carefully preserved between the stage and the audience.

## Print and the New Order

Within the sphere of print, the New Order government (which ended in 1998 when Suharto stepped down) promoted publications that are in keeping with its ideology, devotion to public safety and to stability, and censored those which diverged from these principles. Indeed, various branches of the government —*Kopkamtib* and *Departemen Penerangan*—removed material deemed a threat to the welfare of the nation from circulation and distribution. Books by Pramoedya Ananta Toer were banned; plays by Rendra and Riantiarno were closed down; the news journal *Tempo* lost its publishing permit; articles which described the military actions in East Timor were not published.

There is a very close relationship between print and the national government. Benedict Anderson's book *Imagined Communities* proposes that the birth of the Indonesian nation was made possible through printed newspapers which allowed the individual to imagine thousands of other individuals like himself or herself (Anderson 77). Sylvia Tiwon has furthered the studies of the effects that print literature has had when introduced to orally oriented societies. While print may be, as Benedict Anderson suggests, the stepping stone to nation-building, Tiwon has devoted much of her recent work to examining the deficits in a burgeoning national print culture. In her chapter on the Sundanese rice-harvest rituals, Tiwon demonstrates that within events that have been marginalized by the national culture, such as this ritual performed in a rural village in West Java, women exercise a greater degree of power than they do in the literate, urban spheres.

The nation is continually imagined and re-imagined through the printed texts in the Indonesian language which unify the multiplicity of local cultures under the rubric of a national culture. Education and development, the self-proclaimed central tasks of the New Order government, were accomplished through the introduction of print and print culture into rural sectors, which could then be absorbed into a hegemonic nation. It is useful here to briefly consider the plight of Timor at the hands of the New Order government as an example of how print literature in the Indonesian language is deployed to control the Timorese population. Benedict Anderson notes how the New Order subdued East Timor not only with physical force, but also by establishing Jakarta-sponsored schools throughout the territory. The national education system is the vehicle by which the Indonesian language is introduced. Education thus becomes a double-edged sword in the hands of the New Order government. As Anderson points out in his article "Imagining 'East Timor,'" the Indonesian language learned in the Jakarta-sponsored schools is the means by which the young Timorese are finding "access to the world beyond Indonesia" (Anderson 27). Unfortunately, this access is granted at the cost of local Timorese solidarity.

While the New Order government effectively controlled what was printed and published in Indonesia, making sure that it corresponded properly with the national ideology, what was *not* within this print sphere was able to escape close scrutiny and direct regulation. Local ritual, while influenced by print, was not completely contained within its sphere, and therefore enjoyed a degree of freedom from the responsibility of reflecting the national devotion to security and public safety.

With this in mind, I have included descriptions of rituals which I filmed in their entirety. These rituals, aimed solely at a local and participating congregation, continue to afford a place for those events that are deemed chaotic and disorderly within print-oriented contexts. I also provide descriptions of tourist rituals and films which attempt to represent these rituals to national and international audiences. In these performances, directed at tourist, urban, print-oriented audiences, chaotic events have been eradicated. When these sanitized performances are compared to the local ones, the chaos and disorder of the local rituals stand out.

# THE TWO WORLDS OF BALI

There have been many formal, academic discussions in which analysis of ritual has taken place. Print and print-based terminologies have been employed to represent ritual to a variety of audiences that extend beyond local congregations. Such print-representations include Dutch colonial scholarship, the work done in English by such scholars as Margaret Mead, Jane Belo, Walter Spies, and Clifford Geertz, as well as the countless Indonesian national seminars on culture conducted in the Indonesian language, which have resulted in the official body of knowledge drawn upon for tourism and for Indonesia's education system.

The series of seminars on Balinese culture that began in Bali during the early 1970s have had a tremendous impact on how ritual was represented in academic spheres. A seminar held in March, 1971, entitled *'Seminar Seni Sakral dan Profan Bidang Tari'* (*'Seminar on Sacred and Profane Arts in the Field of Dance'*), formalized the relationship between Balinese culture and *'kesenian'* ('art'). From this seminar a body of knowledge was produced, drawing largely on the work of foreign scholars, in which *'seni sakral'* ('sacred art') was distinguished from *'seni profan'* ('profane art'). Experts from the Balinese academies as well as government officials from local and national offices used the Indonesian language in such seminars and in all the concomitant publications. This seminar was devoted to classifying different types of Balinese dance performance, as well as strengthening the link between the Balinese beliefs and practices expressed by those performances with the central tenet of national tradition and Pancasila: *gotong royong* or community service.

Another seminar, entitled *'Sumbangan Nilai Budaya Bali Dalam Pembangunan Kebudayaan Nasional'* (*'Contributions of Balinese Cultural Values to the Development of National Culture'*), was held more recently in 1986. The Governor of Bali at the time, Ida Bagus Oka, as well as the rector of the Conservatory for the Arts (STSI), Dr. I Made Bandem, presented speeches, which were bound together and published by the Department of Education and Culture (Bagus). Their speeches acknowledged the contributions of foreign scholars, singling out the work of Clifford Geertz on more than one occasion. Once again, *gotong royong* was championed as the essential quality of Balinese culture. Indonesia's national culture thus legitimized itself by claiming it cohered and unified multiple local cultures, Bali among them.

To measure just how much impact such seminars have had, it is interesting to compare the different roles a Balinese *'pemangku'* ('priest') adopted within a ritual I attended June 20, 1995, and at an interview I had with him a week after the ritual. In the ritual, the *pemangku* appeared to be filled with authority, overseeing the prayers held within the temple, accompanying the various masked characters to the stage where the dance-drama was held, and conducting prayers after the dance-drama had ended. In the ritual he was invested with authority and knowledge, reinforced by his titles as *pemangku* and official care-taker of Pura Warung, the temple where the ritual was held.

In the interview, however, he was quite the opposite. He depre-
cated his own authority, and told me I should talk to somebody
from the Conservatory (STSI) who knew more about the ritual. He
shifted nervously as he gave answers which he seemed to feel were
insufficient. I knew I was asking difficult questions when I asked,
for example, what the relationship was between the Barong dance
ritual and the Hindu religion. To questions such as this I would
receive a blank look, a nod, or nothing at all. Often, to a question
about a particular action by a character which seemed rich with
symbolic meaning, I would merely get the reply, "That's the way it
is done."

It is important to point out that the interview took place in Bahasa
Indonesia, the national language of Indonesia, and not in Balinese.
What I was asking the priest to do was essentially to translate what
he knew and experienced in the Balinese language into Indonesian. His struggles with my questions are less a result of his lack of
knowledge on the subjects I posed to him, than of the difficulty
which lies in translating the local knowledge of the Canggu village
into the Indonesian language.

The priest was not educated in the national government's official
interpretations of Balinese ritual, or the government's printed
rhetoric. But he was perfectly aware that such a formalized body
of knowledge existed, and he was familiar to a degree with the
scholarship's terminology. He assumed that it was this body of
knowledge that should be conveyed to me, a foreign scholar
speaking Indonesian. Especially revealing was the priest's decision
to refer to the ritual once as a *slametan* and again as a *'tarian sakral
Barong'* ('sacred Barong dance').

*Slametan* rituals figure very importantly in how foreign scholars
and the national government (which has been influenced heavily
by these scholars) have constructed, or re-constructed, local ritual.
A large body of print-based knowledge, published by scholars such

as Clifford Geertz, describes the Javanese *slametan*. Translated into Indonesian, constructions by these scholars have contributed to the schemata by which local cultures are understood, interpreted, and reconciled with national values such as *gotong royong*. The priest's use of the modern Indonesian terms "tarian sakral Barong" demonstrates the impact that the national seminars described above have had on shaping a body of knowledge devoted to re-representing the ritual. A term the *pemangku* might have used had he been speaking to another Balinese is *mecaru*, which is the term for purification ritual or sacrifice in Balinese.

The *pemangku*'s son joined us midway through the interview. With a confident "selamat malam" ("good evening"), he sat down next to his father and lit a cigarette. He was in his mid-twenties. He received his bachelor's degree in political science from a university in Denpasar, where he had also studied religion privately with an instructor from a religious school. As the interview continued, an interesting dynamic developed between the father and son as they were confronted with my questions. Although both were seated in front of me, I continued to direct my questions to the *pemangku* with whom I had made the appointment. Often, however, after listening to his father's response to my questions, the son would shake his head in apparent disgust, but offer no alternative answer. The son began to cue his father with answers, as his father pondered the question. When I asked the *pemangku* what the poles placed at the corners of the stage represented, the son audibly replied "weapons." The *pemangku* then answered my question in a complete sentence, merely re-stating what his son had told him: the poles were weapons. When I asked the *pemangku* why the Barong had fallen over in apparent defeat, the son answered for him, explaining that although the Barong had appeared to be defeated, he could not be destroyed.

The *pemangku*'s son took charge of the discussion. To a question regarding the large striped flags Rangda is seen carrying, he contradicted his father. The father stated that these are weapons Rangda possesses before she leaves her place of origin to come to the temple space. The son interrupted the father, stating that the flags are symbols which associate her with a dragon, and represent her ability to fly. Thus the son's answer delved into the metaphorical significance of the flags, while the father's statement emphasized the immediate use these flags play within the plot. In other words, the son focused on symbols, a print convention (Havelock 215-233), while the father focused on function. The orientation the son displays towards print became evident at this point, especially since his interpretation can be traced to Walter Spies and Beryl de Zoete's description of the Barong dance-rituals in their well-known book *Dance and Drama in Bali*. As the son took over the responsibility for answering my questions, his statements began to fit a very familiar pattern. The Barong was the representation of good; Rangda, evil.

As has been mentioned, much has been written by foreign and Indonesian scholars on the Barong dance-drama. Central to foreign scholarship has been the portrayal of this dance-drama as the epic struggle between good and evil. The son's authority during the interview, marked by his interruptions and his dismissals of his father's explanations, was derived from his knowledge of the scholarship that has been published on this subject. The son's use of the word "epic" demonstrates his orientation to the print-based categories that describe this ritual. Rather than revere his father's orally derived knowledge of the ritual, which appeared to diverge in telling details from the standard print-knowledge, the son suppressed it, in favor of widely disseminated print interpretations of the Barong. Integral to the son's portrayal of the dance-drama was the care with which he attempted to link the Canggu version of this ritual with the scholarship that has been done on the characters Rangda and Barong. The interview demonstrates two spheres of knowledge which coexist-exist in Bali: the local sphere, which is orally oriented, and the larger macro culture of the nation, which is print-oriented.

The difference between these two spheres is highlighted by the different interpretations of the Barong dance-dramas they yield. Colonial scholars such as Margaret Mead, Beryl de Zoete, Walter Spies, and Jane Belo treat Rangda as the villain and the Barong as the hero. De Zoete and Spies declare this polarity with statements such as the following: "[The book of magic's] teaching was good, but Calon Arang had turned it all to evil by doing everything to left instead of right" (Spies 117). Mpu Baradah becomes the hero in Spies and de Zoete's summary, which refers to him as a "saint." Conceptions of Rangda become even more extreme in the work of Jane Belo, the author of *Bali: Rangda and Barong*. Belo describes Rangda in the following way:

> Whatever turn events may take, she will be evil, she will be female, she will be angry, she will destroy, she will behave like fear incarnate. And you cannot kill her. (Belo 19)

I Made Bandem's work, which is sensitive to the oral discourse of ritual, throws the statements made by Jane Belo and other colonial scholars into question. He has attempted to place Rangda into the context of the ritual, thereby providing his readers with an analysis of the dance-dramas as they appear in the orally oriented sphere. He then states just the opposite of what most foreign scholars have written. Rangda is not the evil villain, but the heroine. In his work *Kaja and Kelod,* I Made Bandem claims that Rangda is actually the savior and protector of the village, because her appearance in the performance is a remedy against black magic: "In Calon Arang, Rangda is the heroine of the performance and represents the protection of the village against the sorcerers" (Bandem 142). Bandem provides additional description of the cultural context:

The Calon Arang play was created to counteract and neutralize the supernatural power of black magicians who are specific individuals in the community. The headquarters for magic, black and white, is located in a small number of coastal villages, like Sanur, Ketewel, Matolan, and Lebih, situated at the kelod [southern] extreme of Bali across from Nusa Penida, the traditional haunt of devils... In the performance of the dance-drama the Condong [maidservant] plays a key role; it is she who explains to the public who is practicing what kind of magic, and how their spells can be counteracted. Then the Rangda and the dusang [corpse] challenge the magicians to throw their worst at them. When the Rangda dancer and dusang survive unscathed at least a temporary respite from sorcery has been won.

According to I Made Bandem, when we see Rangda as the villain, Rangda loses all of her "usefulness" to the villagers and becomes nothing more than an evil witch. He argues that such demoniza-tion of Rangda fails to convey her complexity as a character. She is destructive, but absolutely essential to ridding the village of sorcery. In a separate interviewI Made Sidia, who has played Rangda in traditional performances of the Calon Arang, recon-structed the dialogues which occur between Rangda and the court minister (or Mpu Baradah). The following lines support I Made Bandem's contention that Rangda is the savior of the village, and therefore not the villain of the performance. Often, after she has driven the minister away, she will address the audience of the performance directly. Part of her monologue, spoken in Bahasa Kawi and translated into English, is as follows:

Kawi:

*Ah... kita buta, kala, jin, setan, liak, memedi, aywa kita mang duh enak temugakena ke kikianta lawan yateki Walu Nateng Girah.*

*Aywa amejahaken wong tan weruhing paran paran.*

English:

All of you, buta, kala, jin, setan, liak, memedi [all of these terms connote various kinds of evil spirits or demons] don't go far. Try your strength against the Widow of Girah. Don't kill innocent people, who don't know anything.

My interview with the priest and his son delimits two spheres: the oral and the literate. It is useful to see the ritual itself as belonging to the oral sphere, in which the Barong dance-dramas are recreated with tremendous variation from locality to locality within performance. In the oral sphere of the ritual itself, the *pemangku* demonstrated the highest position of authority, deriving his authority from his many years of experience as a priest in that particular location. In the ritual he barked orders and gave signals to attendants—his son among them—who carried them out promptly. However, in the interview, the *pemangku* found himself posited within the print-oriented sphere my questions invoked, because they were asked in Indonesian, because I was a foreign audience, and because I solicited interpretations. When I asked the priest to interpret, I was asking him to engage in the same process Clifford Geertz refers to as "rationalize" (Geertz *Interpretation* 170-183). His authority was diminished tremendously. The ease with which the son was able to interpret and "to rationalize" his own culture inverted the authority derived from the traditional hierarchy of priest and attendant, father and son. In this particular interview, the son reacts to his father's inability to interpret Balinese culture. The son's orientation to print links his stance to those taken by multitudes of writers in Indonesia. Many writers, as will become evident in the next section, champion education and development and adopt critical stances against those preliterate elements they label as "ignorant."

Colonial scholarship has sought to draw universal statements from the variety with which scholars were undoubtedly faced. By fixing Rangda with one moral and symbolic register, evil, print's affinity for reading objects and characters as symbols does away with the fluidity of Rangda's character. Her paradoxical capacities to destroy and to purge become reduced into pure toxicity. The fluidity Bandem ascribes to Rangda is thus frozen by print conventions, much in the same way that the fluid, permeable stage of ritual drama is contained by the barrier between the stage and audience.

# TWO WORLDS COLLIDE

John Pemberton's book *On the Subject of 'Java'* demonstrates the interaction between the oral and literate spheres. Central to the book is Pemberton's assertion that ritual is undergoing vast change due to the influence of the New Order government during the past thirty years. In his discussions of ritual, Pemberton's main assertion is that those aspects of ritual that may be deemed "disorderly" or even "chaotic" were not in keeping with the New Order's commitment to national stability, and were therefore being suppressed and removed from the ritual context.

Recognizing the role that print and print culture have played in the transformation of ritual actually makes the arguments put forward by Pemberton more convincing, for although he makes it perfectly clear why "disorder" in ritual is being suppressed, he does not elucidate how this change was being enacted. He never mentions whether or not there were military troops or police officers enforcing New Order policy. He never describes the process by which these rituals were restructured to purge them of disorder and chaos. The suppression of "disorder" remains in his book largely a miraculous accomplishment of the hegemonic national rhetoric and its appeal to public safety, development, and the propulsion of Indonesia into the technical era.

Pemberton's book challenges Clifford Geertz's conception that the village *selamatan* is constructed around "self-restraint." In his chapter on village cleansing, Pemberton focuses on the element that has been missing in the essays on Javanese society: *'rebutan'* ('contestation').

> To the limited extent that a *slametan* may be characterized as a communal feast, it represents a feast that is truly, as Geertz notes, furtive. Feasting at a *slametan* usually involves little more than a few quiet bites before departing with a packet of one's remaining portion, for the *slametan*'s focus is the distribution of exchanged food. Rather than a form of communal bonding, *slametan* are, in practice, more of a ritual take-out. What, thus, attracts Javanese villagers to *slametan* is not so much the possibility of feasting together but the promise of returning home with a designated portion of empowered *slametan* food: *berkat*. This *slametan* reward is the product of an exchange that collects pairs of trays from village households, redivides the food collected, and then redistributes some, but not all, of the food in individual trays or packets... Moreover, within the context of a *bersih desa* [village cleansing], the *slametan*'s production of surplus is similarly juxtaposed to the powers of dissemination inherent in acts of *rebutan* by means of a struggle at the site of the village *dhanyang* [guardian spirits]. And it is precisely this juxtaposition that activates Sri—prosperity—and renders the relationship between *slametan* and *rebutan* events not only compatible but necessary. The *rebutan* supplements what would otherwise remain an isolated, somewhat repressed scene of furtive bonding in the form

of a classic *slametan,* and resecures *slametan* practices from their potentially enframed status as a model of *slamet*—a state of security in which "nothing happens"—by implicating them in a broader, intensely active, process of production. (Pemberton 246)

Pemberton describes the tension that exists between the notions of *selametan,* devoted to the orderly distribution of food, and *rebutan,* which is characterized by outright rivalry between village members.

Occasionally the pull towards *rebutan* interrupts even the *slametan* proper, and the *slametan* itself gives way, almost uncontrollably, just as prayers are completed and villagers surge forward to get a handful of the *slametan* food. (246)

Pemberton describes how the New Order philosophy changed village *selametan.* Pemberton cites examples of the replacement of *tayuban* with "orderly male choirs" (247) thereby avoiding the *rebutan* for the sake of security. The exchange of food is no longer an exchange. Families now bring food to the blessings, and receive exactly the same food they have contributed. The shadow-plays, a possible focus of the Javanese ceremony, once an offering in themselves and the site for the redistribution of food, are now framed within the context of providing a useful lesson.

*Rebutan* refers specifically to a time in which participants struggle to obtain a shred of food or perhaps a handful of holy water that has been blessed during the ritual. The video series *The Ring of Fire* contains footage of one such occurrence, when water that has been used to bathe the court weapons is brought to the gates of the *kraton,* where people are eagerly waiting. They scoop handfuls of the water into their mouths and over their heads, pushing and jostling others who seek precious drops that have been imbued with the power of the weapons. *Rebutan* occurs in Bali as well, usually involving a whole roast suckling pig, which is torn apart in a rush of participants who wish to obtain shreds of the blessed meat. In Bali this is not usually referred to as *rebutan*, but *'pemberian'* ('giving'). It still occurs regularly at the mother temple of Bali, Besakih.

Pemberton's argument expands the scope of *rebutan* to include all aspects of the ritual that are deemed chaotic, for the suppression of *rebutan* signifies the suppression of all aspects which do not belong in the carefully arranged processions and performances which now characterize ritual in the urban centers of Central Java. It is not merely the *rebutan* that has been removed from ritual, but all aspects of chaos, struggle, and disorder. In such a manner, "tradition" becomes a construction with which to validate stability under the New Order government.

As previously mentioned, Pemberton does not directly discuss the means by which these suppressions of disorder and chaos have been accomplished, but merely attributes them to the New Order government. In fact, we can sense the difficulty Pemberton faces when he attempts to support his assertions with an account of an actual village cleansing ritual. Rather than referring to details from a direct description of the ritual, he employs a news article which has provided coverage of a ceremony in the village of Tulakan. In this ceremony, *'jembul'* ('plumes') are used to decorate the food offerings. Pemberton makes the following analysis of the news article:

> What remains of the annual jembul encounter is, again, the somewhat eerie juxtaposition of a well-ordered formal procession on the one hand and the deferred pleasure of rebutan on the other hand, an act of ritualized waiting buoyed by an air of intense expectation. The news report notes further that the "air of disorder" (*suasana kacau*) that once surrounded the jembul now

rarely occurs: "What occurs instead is only a parade formation. Thus the onlookers do not really let their emotions explode." What makes this modified jembul procession especially appealing to government officials, thus, is not simply the parade spectacle itself but the spectacle of a rebutan successfully suppressed, a desired incident ritually overcome in the name of "tradition." (255)

We find the journalist defensively insisting that the ritual was "orderly," as if attempting to dispel doubts that arise in the reader's minds about the ritual. Pemberton also provides us with the quotation in which the ritual structure is referred to as a "parade," which apparently helps to create the impression that the ritual was actually an orderly event in which there were clearly defined participants, and a clearly defined group of spectators who we assume passively consumed the event, never letting their "emotions explode." In these glimpses of the news item we see the care the journalist has taken to instill the ritual with the values condoned by the New Order.

While on one level, this article reinforces Pemberton's assertions, it also demonstrates the persistence of the close association of chaos with ritual. Pemberton's choice to include a news article about the ritual rather than observations he made himself demonstrates that it is much easier for him to prove his point within the sphere of print. Very clearly, within this article, "order" is treated as the proper aim for ritual, while "chaos" is something of the past. But these are the values shared within print by Indonesia's readership, and not necessarily the participants of the ritual. Pemberton also makes the following statement about the news item: "As the news reporter cannot help but observe, however, such an incident is precisely what the villagers seem to be waiting for..." (255). Here Pemberton presents the journalist casting the spectators outside of the values championed within the article. Exactly how the journalist was aware that the spectators were awaiting some type of incident is never made clear by either the journalist or Pemberton. But the difference between the postulated audience of the article, and the audience attending the ritual could not be greater. The journalist's readership is assumed to share the ethical stance taken against even traces of disorder, while the spectators are character-ized as desiring chaos.

# TOURISM AND QUESTIONS OF
# AUTHENTICITY IN BALI

Pemberton's analysis would lead one to believe that ritual has transformed completely and permanently from orally oriented events into polished, structured performances void of disorder and chaos. However, my observations of ritual in Bali lead me to believe that the transformation has not been so complete and clean. The rituals that I attended in Bali definitely displayed some tendencies towards a more "orderly" performance, but I noted that there were also strong resistances to such transformations.

Even within Pemberton's analysis, evidence can be found to support the contention that it was the appropriation of print conventions, rather than an alignment with New Order ideologies, that produced change in ritual. Pemberton's description of a wedding ritual, rather than demonstrating ritual performers' response to a decree made by the New Order government, instead reveals the changing tastes of Central Java's urban audiences as they orient themselves to the conventions of print. Rather than the New Order itself, it is the introduction of the 'stage' ('panggung') into ritual which is inhibiting disorder (see Picard 56). Pemberton describes the new presence of chairs available to the guests who come to the ceremony. He acknowledges the power of these chairs which he states, "lies in their disciplining ability to sustain an overall appearance of order" (Pemberton 224). Thus the space of the person who comes to a wedding ceremony has been confined to the chair provided to him; his role is that of witness to the event. Intimately linked with the introduction of chairs into the ceremony is the emergence of the master of ceremonies, who narrates from an unseen place the course of events in the ritual, as it unfolds. The master of ceremonies reads a text which corresponds to the events of the ritual, thereby satisfying the new expectations. A narrative with few slippages between word and action creates the sense that the course of the ritual is completely under the control of the written word, making it possible for it to be performed again and again in exactly the same way.

In Bali, dramas performed exclusively for tourists display many similarities with the rituals that Pemberton describes. The tourist dramas, since they represent the Balinese and Indonesian cultures to more than 800,000 tourists every year, not only demonstrate that the Balinese are fully capable of producing neat and tidy versions of "tradition", but also that they are familiar with the expectations of a print-oriented audience. The ritual, actually a blend of prayer and performance in the temple, becomes purely a performance in the tourist productions, structured just as a theater company might produce a play or opera.

In this portion of my discussion, I will examine Barong dramas prepared specifically for consumption by tourists. I will also present three interviews that may be interpreted as counter-discourses to the trend these tourist dramas have come to represent. What begins to emerge is a very complex picture. Rather than a linear progression away from the oral towards the orderly, literate performance, the relatively new expectations of Indonesia's print culture and the schema by which orally oriented performances are produced and consumed constitute two forces that coexist, each exhibiting its own pull on the ritual.

## The "Tourist" Barong

At one tourist performance I attended, I was handed a photocopied sheet, which contained the plot of the Barong drama that was to be presented that morning. The photocopy contained an illustration of the Barong gamboling across the top of the page. Then the text began. The first paragraph told me that the drama enacted the eternal struggle between good and evil. The Barong was good, while Rangda was his evil opponent. This particular Barong dramatized a story from *The Mahabharata*. As the audience was seated, the musicians, uniformly dressed in bright pink shirts and black sarongs, took their places at the gamelan orchestra on the side of the stage. A few tourists hurried to find their seats. A hush fell over the audience. The music started. The Barong ambled out and the drama began. As the story unfolded, the observer could follow along with his or her handout and know what was happening. The tourist handout divided the performance into five acts, and noted that a musical overture would be given at the beginning. Dewi Kunti was made to sacrifice her son, Sadewa. Rangda, in this story, was the evil witch to whom Dewi Kunti has promised her son. In the final scene, Sadewa, who has been granted immortality by Siwa, transformed into the Barong and fought Rangda. Followers of the Barong, each holding a *kris*, appeared. When they tried to attack Rangda, she turned them against themselves, and the drama ended with a classic picture of the Balinese men each winding his *kris* against his own chest, and each with a dramatic expression of agony bared towards the audience. The music stopped, and there was applause. The audience quietly filed out to where their tour guides, or drivers, awaited them.

## The "Calon Arang" Video Drama

In the United States there are several film versions of the Barong dramas available. They are similar to the tourist performance, providing the viewer with textual explanations of the events as the drama runs its course. The *JVC Anthology of World Music and Dance Video Series* features a Calon Arang drama, which again involves the conflict between the Barong and Rangda. This drama, prepared for consumption by foreign audiences, comes complete with textual explanations which flash at the bottom of the screen as the drama unfolds.

In this video, as in the tourist performance, the musicians appear in uniform. The camera moves in and out to provide the viewer with optimum views of efficiently choreographed scenes. Several times the camera pans down the costumes of the women dancers to allow the viewer to appreciate the beauty of both the dancers and the costumes. Special attention appears to have been given to the choreography of the fight between Rangda and Maling Maguna, who plays a part similar to Mpu Baradah and who is transformed into the Barong in this story. Rangda, with stylized motions, swings her cloth back and forth, systematically driving Maling Maguna down the steps and away from her. The struggle between them is void of any faltering, or losses of balance, producing a scene which is symbolic of a struggle rather than actually a struggle itself. Maling Maguna flees and is replaced by the Barong. The drama runs to its scripted end in which Rangda and the Barong leave the stage together. Although Rangda and the Barong are not seen to engage in any conflict, the text at the bottom states that "the battle between good and evil continues without end."

Both the tourist performances in Bali and the video version of the Calon Arang create a tight correspondence between printed text and performance. Barong and Calon Arang dramas become seamless, unified entities which can be repeated over and over in exactly the same way. The tourist performance becomes an arena in which all of the questions are answerable, all of the sources are clear, and the story is a recognizable one carrying the epic weight of the *Mahabharata* tradition behind it.

## What is Real?

In Bali, disorder and even violence have come to be the mark that distinguishes ritual performances given in rural areas from the tourist performances for national and international audiences. I have collected several statements in which Balinese individuals question the authenticity of the tourist representations of the various rituals. Overwhelmingly, there is the notion that a Barong is 'frightening' (*'ngeri'*), while the tourist version of the Barong is not. I overheard one woman trying to coax her friends into coming with us to a Calon Arang at her temple in Ubud. She described the 'demons' (*'leyak'*) that would be represented in the play. She became very animated as she spoke of the *'kris* attacks' (*'ngurek'*). Further, she poured scorn upon the tourist performances, claiming that they were nothing like the real thing. "A real Calon Arang," she added, "always has a real 'corpse' (*'mayat'*) that they dig up from the graveyard and bring right onto the stage during the performance." She folded her arms, imitating a person shivering with fright.

The Calon Arang ritual which she was describing never employs a real corpse. She was referring to a *dusang*, which is a living man who willingly climbs inside a gunny-sack and feigns death for the course of an entire evening. Crucial to her representation of the ritual as frightening, even dangerous, and thus more valued, is her assertion that the corpse is real. Her comments demonstrate an incredible polarization between the tourist performances in which everything is deemed "fake" and the actual ritual itself, in which she contends everything is "real", even the "corpse" used in the dance-drama.

The different contracts between the performers and the audience is at the heart of the dichotomy between the print-oriented performance and the traditional ritual drama. A basic premise of Greek and of all Western drama has been the assumption that drama imitates reality, and does not constitute reality itself. In fact, Aristotle's *De Poetica* begins with the statement that poetry and drama are modes of imitation. In drama, the audience is transported into a world in which their disbelief is suspended, and in which the author's creation of aesthetic truth temporarily displaces reality for the duration of the performance.

The separation of the audience from the performance in the print-oriented mode becomes a necessity, given that the stage represents an imitation of reality—a fiction—that is, by definition, a detachment from the audience's time and space. The basic aim of ritual drama, however, is not to separate the performance from the congregation for whom it is given. Performances in ritual dramas traditionally have not been consumed as fictions. The performances do not necessarily represent fictive worlds that are separated from the spectator.

What distinguished the tourist performances from the ritual performances for two other individuals with whom I spoke was precisely what Pemberton claims was suppressed by the New Order: those aspects of the ritual deemed disorderly, chaotic, or violent. A gamelan player at a Calon Arang performance I attended at Payungan, prior to the event, told me that this particular evening's performance was not going to be a "good" one, because the '*kris* attacks' ('*ngurek*') would be left out. He could not tell me why, except that the decision had been made at the banjar meeting. What is interesting about his statement was his association of a "good" example of the Calon Arang with the most "chaotic," and apparently frightening, part of the drama-ritual. The absence of *ngurek* undermined the authenticity of the performance for this gamelan player, in spite of the fact that it was being given after midnight in an inner temple, under the supervision of priests.

In an interview with Ngurah Harta, who regularly performs the role of *dusang*, he noted that being a *dusang* has become a profession in Bali. Ngurah Harta is sought by villages from all over Bali for his services. It is not his sole profession, for he is the headmaster of a large martial arts organization. In the interview, he pointed out that traditionally the *dusang* was not a hired professional; only in the past fifteen years have he and other professionals received a salary. He stated that hiring a *dusang* from outside of the village results in a more "violent and dangerous" ceremony. According to Ngurah Harta, the members of the corpse-bearing procession are much more inclined to inflict physical abuse on a hired professional than on a volunteer from their own village. The procession begins at a designated location, then proceeds first to the inner temple, and then ends in the graveyard, where the *dusang* lies in the sealed gunny sack until dawn. Part of being a professional *dusang* is withstanding the kicks, punches, and blows inflicted upon one's body as it is twisted, turned, and even thrown about. Thus we find three individuals associating the authentic ritual with *ngurek*, and the presence of the *dusang*, both of which are markedly altered or absent within the context of the tourist performances. All three of the individuals that were interviewed object to the removal of those very elements that make ritual seem "chaotic and disorderly."

In light of the observations that I made during three Balinese rituals, Pemberton's characterization of ritual applies less to Indonesia as a whole than to the urban, literate spheres of Central Java, where he did his fieldwork. All three of the rituals which I attended took place in rural areas of Bali, and are therefore useful contrasts to the rituals described by Pemberton. While *rebutan* did not take place in any of the rituals that I attended, during the *ngurek* and the time when the *dusang* is brought into the stage-space, the audience flooded the stage-area, creating scenes that were remarkably similar to the scenes of *rebutan* which Pemberton believes to have been suppressed by the New Order.

Rather than being suppressed, these instances are given the unique status of being markers for authenticity within ritual. Just prior to these instances, I found the audience preparing itself for precisely what Pemberton claims is no longer permissible within modern society. Everyone rose to their feet. Children, who were allowed to wander and play freely during other parts of the dance-dramas, were gathered together by their parents, and moved away from the stage-area, which was then flooded with members of the congregation as they pushed forwards towards either the *ngurek* dancers as they fell into trances, or the *dusang* as he was dropped in the center of the stage-area.

Other parts of the dance-dramas, which included scenes in which the clowns engaged in long, humorous dialogues and dances by Baris and Telek/Jauk dancers, demonstrated a different conception of the stage area. During such portions of the ritual, the stage was very much like those employed for a modern theater performances. Very noticeably there were times which mimicked the protocol of a modern stage performance, and there were times in which the barrier between the performers and the members of the congregation dissolved to create one unified space shared by everyone present at the ritual.

# OBSERVATIONS AT THREE RITUAL PERFORMANCES

I will now refer briefly to these three rituals in order to demonstrate that the pull from both the literate and the oral schema manifests itself in two different conceptions of the stage-area. During parts of the performance which most closely parallel print-oriented production, in that they are displays of artistic prowess as opposed to spiritual communion, the stage area is off-limits to the members of the congregation. The congregation becomes indistinguishable from an audience at a play given in a theater. However, during the portion of the ritual when the *ngurek* dancers fall into trance, or when the *dusang* is brought onto the stage-space, the stage-area becomes permeable to the congregation, whose members flow onto the stage towards the men in trance and the *dusang*.

## The Stage

The temple stage, the *kalangan*, is a construction which affords both impermeability and permeability. In the Canggu ritual which

I attended, the *kalangan* was merely a rectangular space marked off with large stakes and gas lanterns. The congregation gathered around the demarcated rectangle, and either sat, knelt, or stood as the series of dances unfolded. At the end of this ritual, members of the congregation stood up and moved into the imaginary space as the trance dancers attacked Rangda with their *krisses* and then proceeded to turn them against their own chests (*ngurek*). At the ceremony I attended in Ubud, the *kalangan* had been more elaborately prepared, consisting of a small bamboo fence approximately two feet high which sectioned off a rectangular space which was to be the stage. A roof, from which phosphorescent lights were hung, covered the area demarcated by the short fence. During the *ngurek* portion of the ceremony, as well as the moment when the *dusang* was brought to the stage area, the congregation stepped over the short fence and pressed forwards, actually pushing those in the very front on top of the men who had fallen on the ground in deep trance. However, during the scenes in which the clowns engaged in dialogues, or the Baris dance was performed, the congregation remained seated behind the bamboo fence as if attending a show at a theater.

In the Payungan ritual, there were two stage-areas. One was a permanent, cement structure, elevated above the level of the congregation viewing the drama. The audience sat on a cement area approximately one meter lower than the level of the stage. This stage was quite small and elevated, impeding any invasion by the audience, especially given that the stage would only allow room for ten people. It is more appropriate to refer to this stage as a *panggung*, rather than a *kalangan*, since this stage oriented the congregation to the performance as passive observers. On this stage, the clowns engaged in their bawdy dialogues, and the court figures gave monologues condemning the Calon Arang's evil deeds. The congregation sat on the mats spread over the concrete as they listened and watched.

The *dusang* and Rangda appeared at a nearby stage-area designated by an uprooted papaya tree transplanted in the middle of the courtyard. Twice the audience moved from their seats on the cement platform to relocate themselves around the *kalangan* in the middle of the courtyard. The first instance was to gather around the *dusang* as the procession entered. The second was when the court minister engaged in a dialogue with Rangda who appeared from the temple gates.

At the Canggu and Ubud performances, the *kalangan* was treated by the congregation as either permeable or impermeable at different times during the performance. The single stage employed during these rituals demonstrated both qualities of the *kalangan*, which is permeable to the audience, and the *panggung*, which, for the purposes of this discussion I will treat as impermeable to the audience. There were moments which were indistinguishable from print-oriented performances one might watch at a theater. At other times, the *kalangan* was permeable to the congregation who flooded the stage-area.

Traditionally the *kalangan* has always contained both of these qualities, since ritual is a blend of performance and ritual activity which may be designated as distinct from the performance (Lansing 10). However, given the nature of the three statements which I have collected and included above, and especially given the fact that some rituals are now employing two types of stages to accommodate the different aspects of the ritual, I suggest that the different aspects of the ritual have been aligned with either literate or oral manners of production and consumption. As the print-oriented portions of ritual become more divergent from those that are orally oriented, they are being assigned to separate sites.

## The Canggu "Barong"

On June 20, 1995, I attended a ceremony at the temple Pura
Warung in Canggu, about ten kilometers out of Denpasar. The
climax of the ceremony was a Barong dance, which began after the
members of the village had brought their offerings and prayed at
the temple. Men drank and gambled, while women and children
sat waiting for the dance-drama performance to begin. When the
dance began, the gambling did not stop, although many of the men
approached the area marked off by poles as the stage. The Barong
Ket character was first to dance, sauntering casually onto the stage.
At this point many members of the congregation still wandered to
and from the stage area. Various men were still busy constructing
a cloth gate at one end of the *kalangan* even though the Barong had
already begun to dance. Later it would be through this curtain that
the various *'topeng'* ('mask') characters and dancers would appear.

I have asserted that portions of the drama are oriented to print
conventions, while others are oriented towards orality, or *rasa*. It is
difficult to determine the significance of each detail in the Canggu
dance-drama, but at two key moments mistakes, or accidents,
were made by the performers. The first mistake occurred while
the Barong was dancing. After making various passes around the
stage, the Barong character sat down and danced by raising its
feet. When the front dancer got up suddenly, the back dancer, who
operated the hindquarters of the Barong, was left behind. The
front began to dance away, deserting the still-seated hindquarters.
Several men rose from the congregation of onlookers lining the
stage area, and aided the hindquarters to its feet. "The front is
already up!" one of the men told the hindquarters. The performer
was helped up, whereupon he began to follow the front again.

This response made by the audience to the lack of coordination
between the Barong dancers suggests that they tolerated the

mistake. This response contrasted sharply with an accident which occurred later during the Baris dance. During the Baris dance, one of the leggings of the dancer's costume came undone. The dancer stopped dancing, knelt down, and tried to repair his legging. He gave up trying to repair it, and instead tore it off. He then tried to tear off the other one so that his costume would be balanced. But he did not succeed in freeing himself of the second legging. The congregation laughed and shouted as the dancer struggled for a few moments and then gave up and continued his dance with one legging on and one legging off.

The two distinct responses of the congregation revealed two different contracts between the performers and themselves. The Baris dancer's accident became the focus of ridicule, while the audience tolerated the error which occurred during the Barong's dance. Later in this discussion, I will return to this issue. Possibly the Barong bears a higher degree of status, or is "holier" than the Baris, and therefore the audience refrains from laughing and jeering at him. However, the fact that the Baris dance has become a category in art competitions has been crucial in the re-shaping of the audience's conception of the Baris dance, since the contest in the Balinese Art Festival has injected the relatively new expectations that the Baris be a seamless example of high art.

As the performance progressed, it became clear that these two contracts also manifested themselves in different conceptions of the stage. Following the Telek/Jauk dance, Rangda emerged from behind the curtain. As Rangda stood at the cloth gate, parents gathered their children together and made them sit. The majority of the men who had been gambling now joined the viewers, kneeling behind the rows of people who sat silently on the ground. Rangda emitted a long and eerie shriek and then came out and began to dance slowly around the stage. Rangda circled the stage, using high leg-lifts, and waving a piece of white cloth. While

Rangda continued to dance, the two Barong dancers re-emerged. As they joined the stage, Rangda's dancing slowed. She circled the Barong which became completely still. At this point clouds of incense filled the stage area, reducing visibility. Murmurs were going through the audience and some people began to stand up. All eyes appeared to be on Rangda and the Barong.

With a loud shriek, Rangda swung the Barong by its beard and struck it with her cloth. The Barong collapsed, both dancers appearing to lie unconscious on the ground beneath the elaborate costume. Rangda retreated to one corner of the *kalangan*, driving away the members of the audience who were in the way. Five Priests, each accompanied by several other men, swooped in and hovered over the two Barong dancers. They helped the two men out of the costumes. The men's eyelids fluttered as they appeared to be drifting in and out of consciousness. The man who played the front of the Barong was helped to his feet and handed a *kris*.

Everyone in the congregation was now on his/her feet. My wife, who held the camera, was jostled. At one point she was lifted up off her feet as the congregation rushed away from the Barong dancer who now held the *kris*. The Barong dancer shouted and convulsed in the restraining arms of several men from the congregation. They directed him towards Rangda who stood perfectly still, facing away from the oncoming attack. The Barong dancer holding the *kris* sprang from their arms, ran across the stage shouting, and drilled the *kris* into Rangda's body, twisting the blade. Rangda met the attack passively, and finally brushed her attacker away with her white cloth. The *kris* was taken from this Barong dancer and raised for all to see. It was given to another man who attacked Rangda again. This attack appeared to be more violent. Several members of the crowd screamed. Rangda withstood this attack and two subsequent ones. The *kris* again was lifted high, available for another attacker, but nobody took the *kris*.

Rangda was ushered to the center of what had once been the stage. Now many of the members of the congregation approached the mêlée. Attendants removed the Rangda dancer's mask, and gave him the *kris*. So many people crowded around him that it was difficult to see what was happening. He violently twisted the *kris* against his own chest, while shouting. He collapsed into the arms of several men. The *kris* was taken from him and given to another man, who twisted it against his own body. His twisting seemed particularly violent, producing several screams from the onlookers. Again, attendants took the *kris*.

The performance part of the ritual ended abruptly. While people still wandered about the stage area, roars of motorcycles could be heard as many families began to leave. A small group of people prayed directly in front of the Rangda, Rarung and Barong characters, led by an older priest, referred to as 'Kak Mangku' ('Grandfather Priest'). The old priest poured holy water into the hands of one of the women praying. She rinsed her mouth with it. All the while the three eminent masked characters towered over her and the priest, silently waiting as the prayers were conducted.

The stage in this performance was constantly dissolving and reforming. Before the performance began, some people sat outside the demarcated rectangle, but others walked right through the middle of it, and children were playing there even as the Barong began its dance. During the performance, men would enter the stage, as when the hindquarters of the Barong had failed to stand up and follow the front. When the *kris* attacks began, members from the congregation including some of the women and children rushed toward the men who had fallen in trance. These lunges were inevitably followed by a push backwards as another man took the *kris* with which to attack Rangda.

At times the stage was much more well-defined, and the atmosphere much closer to that of a print-oriented performance, with a barrier separating performers from the audience. This was particularly true during the Baris and Telek/Jauk dances, which followed the Barong's solo. The increased formality of the Baris and Telek/Jauk dances was signaled when the dancers emerged from a "stage-entrance" made out of a curtain and bamboo poles that had been erected while the Barong was dancing. This entrance was in marked contrast to the Barong's casual saunter onto the stage. The audience clearly held the Baris dancer, who made this more formal entrance, to a higher standard than the Barong, shown when they ridiculed his problems with his costume. His performance is expected to be seamless, and he is taken to task for his failure to maintain this.

## The Ubud Calon Arang

I made several similar observations at a Calon Arang ritual I attended in Ubud. The congregation of viewers was significantly larger: there were probably five hundred viewers. I noticed that several tourists had been drawn into the event from the main road, where there are many hotels and *losmen*. At this performance the *kalangan* had been sectioned off with a two-foot tall fence. A structure had been erected from bamboo and coconut fronds to shelter the stage area. Several electric phosphorescent lights had been placed right on the stage area.

A well-defined barrier existed between the audience and the characters, during the initial scenes which included humorous displays of the clownish villagers being taunted by the demon, Kalika, and accounts of the Calon Arang's destruction given by court officials. At one point, between two such scenes, a young man from the audience, wearing jeans, entered the stage. The crowd shouted and laughed at him as he walked towards the middle of the stage, where he began to dance. The woman next to me put her index finger to her brow, a sign that she thought the young man was insane. He was led off the stage by two other men from the audience. At this point, the ritual was indistinguishable from a play given in a theater. To enter the stage-area was to commit an offense.

Two times, however, the entire crowd stood on its feet and rushed forwards onto the stage, pushing the people in front. The first time was when the *kris* dancers went into trance. A circle of people formed around each one as they lay on the ground. The rush forwards had been so great that some of these viewers were being pushed right on top of the *kris* dancers. Subsequently there was a push backwards to create more room for the priest and Barong so that they might move from one *kris* dancer to the next.

Even greater excitement occurred when the *dusang* was brought in by a procession of perhaps fifty men carrying torches and playing percussion instruments. As they carried the body, they twisted and spun it around while shouting boisterously above the sound of their instruments. His body was tossed back and forth over the heads of the bearers. The body fell to the ground once, but was picked up again. I noticed that several men were punching and beating the body with their fists as it remained held over their heads at the stage-area. The body was dumped in the center of the stage, where it remained for perhaps twenty minutes. Again the crowd poured onto the stage, surrounding the priest who had emerged to bless the *dusang* before he was carried away by the throng of men to the cemetery. While the priest was blessing the body, members of the audience pushed forward, and blended with the procession. I heard many members of the congregation muttering "*mayat*" ('corpse') as they pressed forwards to try to see better.

Suddenly the corpse was hoisted back above the heads of the processionists. There was a surge backwards as the throng began to force its way out of the crowd of viewers. Members of the audience had to move back, but few were willing to yield. Even after the procession had left, the audience remained locked together in a standing position, completely covering the stage-area.

# RITUAL AND "ART"

I have included descriptions of these rituals to demonstrate that in Bali, the disorder noted as being repressed by Pemberton in his studies on Java, has persisted in rituals performed in rural villages. It is precisely the audience's ability to enter the stage-area that produces the aura of chaos in the village ritual, while it is the audience's passive consumption of the performance that creates the atmosphere of order in the tourist performances. While my description of these rituals may appear to contradict Pemberton's assertion that chaos and disorder were suppressed under the New Order regime, it must be pointed out that he describes ritual as it takes place in urban settings, in which print culture has had a greater impact on ritual. Therefore my observations may be used to amplify Pemberton's statement. Ritual in Bali changed over the thirty years of New Order rule, not because of a decree suppressing "disorderly and chaotic" elements; it has transformed instead in response to the introduction of print-culture, whose characteristics of performance ritual has, to some extent, appropriated for itself. In fact, the New Order government had a greater effect on ritual through its promotion of literacy than through the physical monitoring and control of ritual by police or military.

The degree to which ritual changed in Bali is indicative of a complex dialogue between the pull towards the future of modern print culture and that towards the past of ritual and orally oriented production. The transformations that I have noticed are far from uniformly leading in a single direction to a "more orderly" atmosphere. Rather, these rituals contain elements of both a print-oriented and an orally oriented production. At certain times the stage is off-limits to the audience, while at others it is appropriate, even inevitable, that the audience pour onto the stage. During the June 20 ritual in Canggu, it was noticeably during the Baris and Telek/Jauk dances that the audience did not intrude upon the stage-area. At the Ubud ritual performance, it was just prior to the entrance of the clowns that the young man was denied access to the stage. I pointed out that the audience responded much more vociferously to the mistake made by the Baris dancer than they did to the mistake made when the front legs of the Barong walked away without his hindquarters. I wish to suggest that this is because the clown scenes and the Baris dance have become much more affiliated with artistic performance, than has the Barong. Here we find the influence of the New Order government. I attribute the different attitude the audience demonstrated during the Telek/Jauk dance to the fact that the Baris and Telek/Jauk dances have become categories for contests during the Bali Art Festival—a government sponsored event—held at the Art Center every June in Denpasar. It is the association of these dance categories with fine art that produces the different mode of consumption, and the new contract with the audience.

## "Art" in Bali

Concurrent with the arrival of print in what was to become Indonesia was the advent of the Western concept of high or fine art. In the Balinese language, there is no such term which can be said to correspond to "fine art." Michel Picard, in his article "Cultural Tourism," writes:

> What we call "art" is for the Balinese a functional occupation, a service to the gods and community, a task which is always concrete and specific, executed by a "specialist." Thus a dancer is a "dance specialist" (*'juru igel'*), while a musician is a "music specialist" (*'juru gambel'*). (Picard 45)

The national language of Indonesia, Bahasa Indonesia, clearly does contain such a concept. The word *"kesenian"* is used to refer to literature, painting, sculpture and theater, which were not necessarily separable categories in Bali, Java, or the Malay World prior to the twentieth century.

Amin Sweeney, in his book *A Full Hearing*, has done much to demonstrate how Dutch and English scholars, heavily influenced by the Romantic Movement in Europe, evaluated and classified cultural elements of the Malay World according to their predefined categories, which included the historical and the romantic narrative. Sweeney has demonstrated that neither of these were distinct categories in the Malay World, and were often found inextricably woven together in a variety of different oral media such as the *hikayat*, the *wayang*, or the *tarik selampit* genre of story-telling (Sweeney 17-43).

With the introduction of tourism into Bali by the Dutch in the early twentieth century, Bali has become a place with diverse audiences, which range from pre-literate Balinese, to educated Balinese, to the Europeans. Over the past seventy years enormous

changes have been made by Dutch and Indonesian national officials to accommodate the flocks of Europeans who began to attend
Balinese dance-dramas and rituals. In the 1930s, Walter Spies was
very influential in the production of new forms of "cultural
performance," taking elements from Balinese ritual and incorpo-
rating them "artistically" in "cultural performances" such as the
*Kecak Fire Dance*. Later Bali received an injection of "art" which
was originally supposed to be performed exclusively for tourists.
The term *"Sendratari "* was introduced in 1961, which Michel
Picard defines as: "an acronym composed from the roots *seni*: 'art,'
*drama*: 'theater,' and *tari*: 'dance.'" (Picard 52). Picard discusses the
difference between the *Sendratari* and the established standards of
ritual performance by pointing out that *Sendratari* fits a Western
notion of performance art. It is meant to be visually consumed on
a stage before a well-defined audience. This "high art" for tourists,
however, has clearly crossed over and made its way into the ritual
performances, resulting in a blending of "performance art" and
ritual. Picard demonstrates the complex relationship between
"performance art" originally designed for non-Balinese audiences,
and Balinese ritual when he discusses Legong dance:

> [T]he fate of the short group dance which opens every
> performance of "Legong dance"—whether destined for tourists
> or for the Balinese—is revealing. It was originally a temple dance,
> called the Pendet, performed by dancers presenting welcoming
> offerings of flowers, food, and incense to the visiting gods
> installed on their shrines. During the 1950's, it became the rule to
> greet President Sukarno and important state guests with a large-
> scale Pendet. This custom was then taken up by the management
> of the Bali Beach Hotel, which decided to open each Legong
> dance with a Pendet, as a welcome dance for their guests. This
> caused great distress to the Balinese religious authorities,
> shocked that the tourists were being treated in the same way as
> the gods, and worried about the desecration of ritual dance.

Thus, in the late sixties, they ordered the composition of a new dance inspired by the Pendet from a choreographer of the Conservatory of Music. Entitled *Panyembrama* (literally 'that which is offered to the guests') or else '*Tari Selamat Datang*' ('welcome dance'), this new creation from then on replaced the Pendet as a curtain-raiser to the tourist performances. Later on, this tourist version of a temple dance was brought back to the temple, as dancers who had learned the Panyembrama at the Conservatory began to perform it instead of the Pendet during temple festivals.... (52)

*Sendratari* has created media to be enjoyed, observed, and evaluated by an audience, rather than shared in a transformative performance. The endeavor to display *Sendratari'*s visual opulence imposes a new set of demands upon the production of rituals. Central among these demands is the need for the dancers and performers to be seen by the audience. Hence, we can understand the pressure for performances to be given on stages (*panggung*) which afford an audience the ability to view the performance, while also greatly restricting the audience's access to the stage.

*Sendratari* is the medium for competitions, which have become more and more common events. Recall here my discussion of the Greek origins of drama, which first introduced the two qualities I have been associating with "print-oriented" production: the primacy of the author, and, most importantly, the role of the audience. This original Greek audience, as I pointed out, was composed of judges, whose task it was to evaluate the merit of the dramas performed in competition before them. Such a judicial role, demanding objectivity, critical expertise, and above all distance, set the terms for the audience of print production: it is an audience that listens and does not participate. As Bali embraces the format of these Greek dramas, the format of competition, the Balinese audience begins to follow the lead of the Greek audiences: they become silent, critical consumers of a performance they recognize as art.

While tourism is frequently cited as having a tremendous influence on the reshaping of Balinese cultural productions, the effect of the multitudes of contests which take place at the state and local levels in Bali has not been examined. The contest is the alternative to 'contestation' (*rebutan*). One critic, Jakob Sumardjo, in *'Pengantar Novel Indonesia'* ('Introduction to the Indonesian Novel'), celebrates the stability which the New Order brought to art, and attributes the new abundance of writers to this stability. According to Sumardjo, the novel blossomed under the care of the New Order, which he proves with simple reference to the fact that in the 1970s more novels were published in Indonesia than in any other decade (Sumarjo xviii). Significantly, he attributes the increase in production to the New Order's sponsorship of literary contests. Once again, competition is identified as the fertile ground, the ideal environment, for the production of art.

*'Adat'* ('Cultural') competitions are an advent of the New Order government (Nordholt 31). Such competitions began even at the village level (*'lomba desa adat'*) concurrent with the passing of the Law on Village Government of 1979 (Warren 241). This law was designed to create uniformity within the village government, but also had the effect of amalgamating villages into larger units (*'kelurahan'*). The *Sendratari* contests have been the means by which the print-oriented mode of consumption were introduced into villages. These contests have essentially placed the Western conception of art and performance alongside the dramatic rituals. Audiences attend a theatrical contest, and the following day attend a ritual; little wonder that the contest and the ritual begin to look more alike.

In the contest, elements of the ritual are separated from one another, and presented as art. In contests, dances are performed with a minimum of prayer. Offerings are displayed like sculptures, to be observed and critiqued as objects of art, whose function is purely aesthetic. Moreover, like the Greek plays that first set the terms of print consumption, the competition is mediated by a group of officially appointed judges. Perhaps more so than in tourism, the contest has produced the need for the creation of categories and the establishment of uniform standards (which have appeared in print) within those categories. In the Denpasar Art Museum one may witness the variety of appearances that different regions once gave to the Rangda mask. One features eyes made out of the bottoms of coke bottles. Now there are specifications as to the size, color, even the materials from which the masks may be produced. Most importantly contests have reinforced the role of the cultural expert who now comprises an important element in the audience and who possesses a scholarly knowledge with which he/she may evaluate culture.

## The Art Center

The Art Center stage, built with complete funding from the government, created an arena for large-scale *Sendratari* performances and competitions for Balinese audiences. This theater combined the Western model of a stage with Balinese elements in order to produce the grandest arena to be found in Bali—a spectacle in itself. The stage is renowned for its beauty and is included in most tourist books on Bali. Outside the open-air theater is a large parking lot and a ticket office. From the parking lot, one may notice the top of a massive Balinese-style temple gate protruding from within the coliseum, giving the impression that an entire temple is contained within. Inside, one immediately realizes that the temple gate is actually the back of the stage, creating a permanent setting, which, when fully lit and beautifully decorated for evening performances, is reflected by the pond which surrounds the stage like a moat. From the pond hundreds of rows of cement benches rise to the lip of the coliseum, providing seating for more than a thousand people. Microphones are hung over the stage so that the large audiences are sure to hear the performance, whether it be the raucous exchanges of the Drama Gong characters, or the music from a Gong Kebyar.

Of the different types of *Sendratari* performed at the Art Center, undoubtedly the most popular is the Drama Gong. Like most *Sendratari* creations it draws on the literary themes of *The Ramayana* and *The Mahabharata*, but is very obviously devoted to parody and farcical buffoonery. Its popularity is indicated by the numerous Drama Gong performances held during the Art Festival. The closing ceremony is always followed by a performance by the winning cast of the Drama Gong competition at the Art Center theater. The Drama Gong was created in 1966 by artists from the Conservatory specifically to entertain large Balinese audiences, and is performed frequently throughout the year at the Art Center theater. Although hundreds of viewers attend, usually purchasing tickets for ten thousand rupiahs (approximately one US. dollar), the performances are often also televised on TVRI Denpasar's station.

The structure of the Art Center theater reveals a devotion to separating the audience from the performance. As if the cement benches and the elevated stage were not impediment enough, there is a moat between the viewers and the performers. The viewers are relegated to the passive roles of watching and evaluating. They are completely prohibited either from entering the stage-space, or participating in the events on the stage. While the content of the Drama Gong is bawdy, as characters often bludgeon each other with inflatable phalluses, or branches of shrubbery, the separation between the actors and the audience is ensured by the very structure of the Art Center itself. Here we witness again the stance print-culture takes against "chaos and disorder," which within the contexts of this discussion specifically refers to an invasion of the stage-space by the audience.

Yet, even at the Art Center, I witnessed the coexistence of the two modes by which performances in Bali are consumed. In spite of the "control" cultivated through the promotion, sponsorship, and funding of print-oriented events by the Indonesian government, the interactive schema by which the ritual is consumed persists, coexistent with the introduction of these relatively new forms enforcing audience passivity and spectatorship. At one Drama Gong I attended in June, 1994, the same interplay existed between the traditional sense of the stage—the permeable *kalangan*—and the new, "Western-style" *panggung*. In this case, the barrier between the audience and the stage was traversed not by an audience flooding onto the stage-space, but by an actor who penetrated the audience.

At this performance, one of the actors walked to the edge of the stage and waved at the audience. "Hello," he shouted. "Hello," some members of the audience replied. The actor stood there with his hands on his hips, comically scrutinizing his audience. He looked from one person to the other, making comments in Balinese, which were met with laughter. Suddenly he feigned losing his footing, dramatically swinging his arms to avoid falling into the moat which separated himself from his audience. This was met with uproarious laughter from the audience. The actor recovered, and again took his pose with his hands on his hips. He studied the audience once again.

"Jump," someone from the audience shouted. And this was met with equally uproarious laughter.

The tension and humor were heightened when the actor pretended to test his leg muscles with his hands. Many were shouting "Jump!" Several young men rushed from their seats and stood on the other side of the water, opposite the actor, encouraging him to jump across to their side.

"All right, I'll do it!" he shouted.

The audience rose to their feet as the actor stood, his toes gripping the edge of the stage, his legs flexing in tandem with his swinging arms. The actor jumped, and came crashing across the moat into the arms of the men on the other side. Pandemonium ensued. People stood on their seats. Many surged down to where the actor stood. Out of the range of the overhead microphones, standing on top of one of the cement benches, the actor continued to shout at the audience in Balinese.

"Again!" the man next to me shouted. "Again!"

This time the actor took a running start and hurled himself back onto the stage. He rolled dramatically and sprang to his feet, his hands immediately shooting back to his hips. He returned to the edge of the stage triumphantly.

"Again!" came a chorus of shouts. "Again!"

And again the actor leaped over the moat into the crowd on the other side.

His return jump produced screams of horror. One of his legs had dipped into the water. He scrambled quickly up onto the stage, holding his knee in apparent pain. There was a brief silence, as he examined his knee. Suddenly he stood upright and smiled. The audience cheered. The actor shook the water off his feet producing laughter again in his audience. He shook his hands over his head like an Olympic champion, prompting another standing ovation. Then the gamelan began and the drama continued. Several times during the performance the actor would suddenly feign a limp which again drew a tremendous response from the crowd.

In essence, this actor temporarily removed the barrier between the audience and the performance. The response from the audience is indicative of the potency of his move, and the effect it had in producing, for a transitory moment, a traditional stage—a *kalangan*—out of the modern *panggung*. When the audience poured down the amphitheater towards the actor, it was as though he had become a magnet for the engulfing audience, much like the dancers who had gone into trance at the rituals I attended.

For a moment the tight seams of the performance came completely undone as the entire amphitheater erupted into pandemonium. Many had left their seats to join the crowd that had gathered around the actor, who was passed around in the hands of the audience before he was allowed to return to his place on the stage. After his return, ushers busied themselves escorting those who had flooded around this actor back to their seats. During the return to the drama, I was aware of an interesting aura that had enveloped the entire arena. The ushers were laughing while they perfunctorily set about restoring order to the performance, as was the entire audience. There was very little sense of danger that the audience was going to lose its control. What had happened was quite obviously inappropriate, but everyone had engaged in the impropriety together. The drama had been temporarily suspended while the entire audience and actor engaged in the activity that was so familiar to everyone at a temple, but out of context at the Art Center. We can imagine if a news article had been written about the event what if might have said. It most certainly would have taken a critical stance against the behavior of both the performer and the audience, lambasting the event as chaotic, primitive, even dangerous.

I included this description to demonstrate that the strong orientation to both print and oral conventions is not just limited to the ritual sphere, but may be seen to shape a wide variety of gatherings in Indonesia. Although the Drama Gong is performed well within the constructs of the print culture, the strong pull of the ritual schemata is present, underlying the formality with which the Art Center is imbued. The Drama Gong actor's leap into the audience disrupted a performance which would have been indistinguishable from Western theater. His leap changed the contract with the audience from that of a print-oriented performance to that of ritual drama. This actor broke the barrier between fiction and reality. The actor's leap, which temporarily reduced the formality of the performance to disorder, while it constituted exactly what the Art Center stage is built to impede, appeared to be precisely what the audience was waiting for.

# CONCLUSION

This chapter seeks to contribute to the studies concerning the various transformations that modernity has brought about within Balinese culture, specifically within the context of ritual drama. Scholars, including Clifford Geertz, Anthony Forge, and John Pemberton, have focused on how the ritual performance is affected by the political climate in Indonesia, thereby linking transformations within ritual production to changes in over-arching political structures. In these studies, the scholars' lenses have been consistently trained on the ritual performances. Seldom included within their scope of examination is the role of the members of the congregation, and their interaction with the performances. Geertz and Forge have pointed out trends of "ratio-nalization" the purpose of which is to legitimize Bali within the Indonesian nation. "Rationalization" is a process of making a fluid collection of diverse local cultures unified, organized, and thus presentable to the Ministry of Religion in Jakarta. Pemberton has examined the suppression of chaos in Javanese ritual as a sign of the tremendous influence that the New Order government has exerted over the Indonesian population. While such analysis brings to light meaningful studies of power structures in Indonesia, these scholars are seldom able to explain precisely how change is effected within the local sectors of the population. The agent of change is always vague and hegemonic.

In this discussion, I have pinpointed the audience's interaction with the performance as the template upon which to examine the changes that are taking place within ritual. I have discussed how modernity has transformed ritual by introducing to ritual print and the print conventions of performance, which has resulted in a new contract being established between the performers and their audience. This contract recasts the audience from the role of participant to that of passive, objective observer. I have pointed out that this print-oriented contract, at crucial times, dissolves and gives way to a different contract, that of ritual drama, in which the audience aggressively interacts with the performance. The two contracts between the performers and the audience, that of print and that of ritual drama, manifest themselves most noticeably in the audience's relationship to the stage, which is at times the well-defined and separated stage of a print-oriented production, and at other times a fluid space permeable to the congregation.

By developing an understanding of the two opposing yet concurrently functioning contracts between the performance and the audience, I have laid the groundwork for an approach to a broad range of topics addressing ritual drama in Bali. The permeability of the stage is crucial in that it removes the distance which the audience requires in order to objectively witness and evaluate the ritual. Therefore, the congregation's access to the stage-space casts the proceedings of the ritual as fact, rather than as dissociated fiction.

My study of ritual drama attempts to widen the frame given to ritual, to expand the scope beyond the edge of the stage to include the members of the congregation. The exclusion of the congrega-

tion limits the study of ritual to the performances. The audience
has been left out, a significant and distorting omission, given the
congregation's uniquely participatory, interactive role with the
performers. By stepping on the stage, the audience members of
ritual drama in Bali become an intrinsic part of the performance,
not just detached observers of it. Margaret Mead and Gregory
Bateson's camera turned its back on the congregation that was
present during their filming. Consequently, Mead and Bateson
recast the ritual drama as a dramatic performance typical of print
convention, to be witnessed by a distant, alienated, and unimpli-
cated foreign audience.

The placement of Rangda within the print sphere of theater, film,
and the written word has laid her out for all to scrutinize, in some
cases a bit like a noble animal caged in a zoo. She has been choreographed for tourists, manipulated by state power, and demonized
from multiple perspectives including foeign scholars and authori-
ties of other religions, namely Christianity and Islam. In some
ways, the course of this book would lead one to believe she is in
danger of being marginalized further and further to more remote
and more isolated spaces in the temples of forgotten villages, left
behind in the mad rush to develop, modernize, and become tech-
nically savvy and globally competitive. And yet, with the very
resilience and capacity to renew that she encapsulates, even within
the patriarchal print-sphere that was the very trap in which her
submission was achieved, she has been able to resurrect herself in
all of her glory and power.

As mentioned in the first chapter, modern Indonesian writers have
loosened the chains that have bound her into compliance with
New Order policies. Goenawan Mohamad, Toeti Heraty, and Cok
Sawitri were inspired by her to tell their own stories just as I was
with my personal anecdote. As mentioned in the first chapter,
their stories, much more so than mine, treat the epic as fluid and
dynamic, and, whereas I, a "white teller" telling a "brown story,"

treated the story as fixed and static, each of them saw it as an invitation to reimagine the events surrounding a single mother living in the village of Girah, to question the transmission of the story as it was made to serve political power, and finally to free Rangda from the stigma with which she has been branded. .

The scholar, Curnow, mentioned in the first chapter discusses each of these Indonesian writers in her dissertation. Mohamad wrote a libretto for an operetta, "The King's Witch," in which he imagines how the voices of the villagers would have told a different story, who may have seen her in a more favorable light as a maternal figure maligned by the "mendacious political denials of Mpu Baradah and the anguished, defeated voice of the king" (Curnow 37). Toety Heraty explores the possible historical distortion of the widow figure by fixing her within the stereotypical dichotomy of women into virgin and nurturing or promiscuous and destructive. Curnow writes:

> In Toeti's prose lyric, each of the 18 chapters has a different theme, for example, Calon Arang in Balinese Culture; Calon Arang according to Literary Research; Misogyny and Patriarchy; and so on. It therefore resembles a book of essays in poetic format, with academic asides. In contrast to the libretto by Goenawan Mohamad (a critique of state power through the Calon Arang legend), the scope of Toeti's prose lyric is more ambitious; it is a series of feminist vignettes, each examining a particular aspect of patriarchy. (41)

The third writer, Cok Sawitri, was inspired by political events to create her rendition of the epic, titled *Pembelaan Dirah,* which might translate to "Guardian of Dirah (Girah)." Just from the title one can sense that Sawitri attempts to recover the nurturing, moral, and creative power of a mother goddess figure who has been stripped of her memory by patriarchal history. Curnow writes: "According to Sawitri (2004: 9) Rangda was not a practitioner of black magic who worshipped Durga, but the spiritual leader of a religious community in the village of Girah, with many followers. She explains that the marriage of Ratna Manggali to Bahula took place with the blessing of Rangda, who believed that Bahula was a follower of Buddha" (43).

Initiated in the year 1990, *Pembelaan Dirah* is an ongoing, open-ended work, which includes a live performance inspired by the political climate in Indonesia in 1996. This was near the end of the New Order when a challenger of Suharto's bid for presidency, Megawati Sukarnoputri, daughter of the first Indonesian president, Sukarno, began to gain tremendous popularity. She won the position as leader of the Democratic Party of Indonesia, but in a backhanded move, Suharto acknowledged her party rival, Suryadi, as the leader instead. Thus the Democratic Party was split into two groups: PDI-Suryadi and PDI-Mega. Megawati and her supporters refused to yield from the central office in Jakarta. There, music was played and numerous speeches championing democracy and fair elections were given. It was believed to be a peaceful and orderly occupation. It is widely held that Suharto's government organized a crowd of people to dress like PDI-Suryadi supporters and storm the office. The result was two days of rioting in which people were killed, went missing, and were injured. Also importantly, Megawati was discredited through her association with the riots, and her bid for presidency was ended (she would, however, become vice president later in 1999, and eventually, in 2001, the fifth president of the Republic of Indonesia). Barbara Hatley in her essay "Literature, Mythology, and Regime Change: Some Observations on Recent Indonesian Women's Writing," discusses Cok Sawitri's use of *The Calon Arang* epic to illuminate and critique the incident of July 27, 1996 in the following way:

In Cok Sawitri's vision, as in Goenawan Mohamad's libretto, Calon Arang's struggle is not against universal patriarchy but totalitarian state power. The inspiration for this work, the artist reports, was the July 1996 attack by Soeharto regime thugs on the headquarters of Sukarnoputri's [Megawati's] party. For Cok Sawitri, Megawati at this time was a symbol of the nation's suffering—'negeri saya jadi janda' (my country had been made a widow)—abused and marginalised. She studied various versions of the Calon Arang story in palm-leaf manuscripts, developing a view that she had represented a sect that opposed King Erlangga and his priest Mpu Bahrada (sic.) on religious grounds. When attacked by the king, the Dirah group defended themselves spiritually rather than physically, in similar fashion to Megawati's moral and legal resistance to the Soeharto regime after the routing of her party base. The performance drew on several Hindu mantras expressing peace.

Though conceived and developed in 1996, the performance was not presented publicly until 1999. The dangers of taking on and personally re-creating the magically powerful Calon Arang role, heightened presumably by the anti-government, political suggestion of this new interpretation of this new interpretation, were too great. Cok Sawitri fasted for months in preparation for the first performance; her own mother tried to dissuade her, fearing she would die, and huge crowds gathered to watch. By the time of this presentation, in August, Megawati had won a majority in the general elections but was being sidelined in the political manoeuvring for the presidency, as Islamic religious leaders declared illegitimate the concept of a female head of state. By November, when the monologue was performed at the launching of Toeti Heraty's poem, Megawati had lost the presidency to Abdurrahman Wahid. Like Calon Arang, she was experiencing ongoing slander and marginalisation. Cok Sawitri is quoted in a review of the performance as suggesting that her work also has a wider reference: "What I want is for everyone to carry out resistance in her own space".

The association of the Calon Arang myth with Megawati provides an intriguing variation on her usual portrayal in political discourse as 'Ibu' [mother]—both exalted by her followers as nurturant mother of the nation, and scornfully dismissed by her critics as unskilled housewife, unprepared for political leadership. The comparison with Calon Arang rests on Megawati's experience of oppression by a central, patriarchal state, and bears the positive suggestion of a deep-seated power, suppressed all the more ruthlessly because of its threat to the status quo. No direct connection is made in Cok Sawitri's work with the infamous Calon Arang-like images of the monstrous female which the New Order state itself produced and propagated. But new tellings of the tale emerge, and new workings of the image. (Hatley 137-138)

Cok Sawitri, in playing the role of Calon Arang in her performance, is physically reclaiming the role as feminine (a female role played by a woman) rather than a male portrayal of women's energy gone out of control. It was pointed out earlier that the role is assigned to a male (and later in the final chapter we will see how the male should have received a sign from Rangda in their dreams that she has chosen him to play her in village rituals). However, as Mohamad, Heraty, and Sawitri all argue with their retellings of this epic, the male portrayal of Rangda as grotesque and destructive is in alignment with the very patriarchal powers of the state that would be threatened by female creative power as an alternative to its authority. Cok Sawitri takes her retelling one step further by appropriating the traditional role of the male when she takes on the part naturally as a woman, effortlessly emanating maternal, sometimes nurturing sometimes fierce energy. The patriarchal traditions of the past have marginalized women from their own capacity for power and authority within society, and under Sawitri's direction, with Rangda played by a woman rather than a man, they are re-aligned with the very expressions of power and *semangat* featured in Rangda's iconography, from which they have been prohibited. Rangda is no longer an expression of male anxiety over what goes wrong when women are unsequestered, uncontrolled, or given political freedom, but becomes a symbol for a woman's concern for her family and her community, her natural gift for the role of head of household and village, and her willingness to defend them both fiercely.

# WORKS CITED

- Anderson, Benedict. *Imagined Communities*. London: Verso, 1991.
- ----------. "Imagining 'East Timor.'" *Arena Magazine*. April-May 1993
- Bagus, I Gusti Ngurah. *Sumbangan Nilai Budaya Bali Dalam Pembangunan Kebudayaan Nasional*. Jakarta: Departemen Pendidikan Dan Kebudayaan, 1986.
- Bandem, I Made. *Kaja and Kelod: Balinese Dance in Transition*. Kuala Lumpur: Oxford University Press, 1981.
- Belo, Jane. *Bali: Rangda and Barong*. Seattle and London: University of Washington Press, 1949.
- Curnow, Heather M. "Women on the Margins: An Alternative to Kodrat?" Doctoral Dissertation. Tasmania: Hobart School of Asian Languages and Studies, October 2007.
- Forge, Anthony. "Balinese Religion and Indonesian Identity." *Indonesia: Australian Perspectives*, ed. James J. Fox. Canberra: Research School of Pacific Studies, The Australian National University, 1980. 221-33.

- Geertz, Clifford.. "Religious Change and Social Order in Soeharto's Indonesia." *Asia* 27. Autumn 1972. 62-84.
- ----------. *The Interpretation of Cultures.* United States of America: Basic Books, 1973.
- ----------. *The Religion of Java.* Chicago: University of Chicago Press, 1976.
- Hadiwijono, Harun. *Man in the Present Javanese Mysticism.* Baarn: Bosch and Keuning N.V., 1967.
- Hatley, Barbara. "Literature, Mythology, and Regime Change: Some Observations on Recent Indonesian Women's Writing." *Women in Indonesia: Gender, Equity and Development.* Singapore: Institute of Southeast Asian Studies, 2002. 130-143.
- Havelock, Eric. *Preface to Plato.* Cambridge, Mass.: Harvard University Press, 1963.
- Lansing, J. Stephen. *The Three Worlds of Bali.* New York: Praeger Publishers, 1983.
- Nordholt, Henk Schulte. *State, Village, and Ritual in Bali: A Historical Perspective.*Amsterdam: VU University Press, 1991.
- Pemberton, John. *On the Subject of 'Java.'* Ithaca and London: Cornell University Press, 1994.
- Picard, Michele. " 'Cultural Tourism' in Bali: Cultural Performance as Tourist Attraction." *Indonesia.* 49. 1990.
- Pollmann, Tessel. "Margaret Mead's Balinese: The Fitting Symbols of the American Dream." *Indonesia.* 49. April, 1990.
- Schechner, Richard. *Between Theater and Anthropology.* Philadelphia: University of Pennsylvania Press, 1985.
- Spies, Walter and Beryl de Zoete. *Dance and Drama in Bali.* London: Faber and Faber Limited, 1938.
- Sumardjo, Jakob. *Pengantar Novel Indonesia.* Bandung: PT Citra Aditya Bakti, 1991.

- Sweeney, Amin. *A Full Hearing: Orality and Literacy in the Malay World.* Berkeley: University of California, 1987.
- Tiwon, Sylvia. *Women in the Production of Discourse* (unpublished manuscript).
- Turner, Victor. "Dramatic Ritual/Ritual Drama: Performative and Reflexive Anthropology." *The Kenyon Review* 1, no. 3. 1979. 80-93.
- Warren, Carol. *Adat and Dinas.* Oxford: Oxford University Press, 1993.
- Wiryamartana, I Kuntara. *Arjunawiwaha.* Yogyakarta: Duta Wacana University Press, 1990.

# ALSO BY BRANDON SPARS

www.ingramcontent.com/pod-product-compliance
Lightning Source LLC
Chambersburg PA
CBHW021147090426
42740CB00008B/976